# Journeys

***True stories of hope and recovery from those who have lived through an eating disorder***

***A Methodist Hospital Eating Disorders Institute publication***

 For information, contact:
Methodist Hospital Eating Disorders Institute, 6490 Excelsior Boulevard, Saint Louis Park, MN 55426.

http://www.parknicollet.com/edi



Book design by J Campbell, Artville, Inc.

ISBN: 0-9747282-0-9

First edition: May 2004
09 08 07 06 05 04 1 2 3 4 5 6

*This book is*

*dedicated to any person*

*who quietly struggles with*

*an eating disorder.*

# Contents

# Foreword

Living in the world of an eating disorder can be debilitating beyond any stretch of the imagination. For the person enduring the illness, life loses color; companionship and self-identity are often abandoned to keep the eating disorder sustained. For those who are watching the eating disorder taking root in their loved one's mind and body, the loss and grief become almost unbearable. Friends and family long for "normalcy"—a reunion with the person that they all knew before, a return to the life that they all shared and built together.

It is difficult, in the midst of this sadness and yearning, to find even a sliver of light. Recovery is a process that may take many years and traverse countless hills and valleys. Eventually, a person with an eating disorder can heal—and does—but in the process, the path seems so lonely, so darkened by shadows. If you are a person who is living with an eating disorder, you are all too familiar with this pain.

This book is *not* about that suffering. Rather, it is about the hope that materializes on the road toward recovery. Each chapter represents the voice of someone who has gone through an eating disorder—either an individual who has struggled with the illness or a loved one who has witnessed this struggle.*

As these accounts illustrate, there is no right or wrong way to recover from an eating disorder. Some people take on their recovery as though they are at battle—fiercely fighting to bring the "normal" back into their lives. Others are more deliberate with their healing—taking time to journal about their experiences and to analyze the effect of what it may mean to be permanently free of the disorder.

How long it takes to recover is also not an easy issue to address. Some individuals are completely free of eating disorder symptoms within one year of beginning treatment. Others, however—including some people presented in this book—grapple with an eating disorder for years, even after seeking treatment.

The point is, every journey toward recovery is intensely individual and filled with opportunities for growth, reflection, and self-revelation. The ultimate gift of a healing odyssey lies in the fact that no one but you can walk the path.

The recollections contained in this book are raw and humble, as each person details how the eating disorder consumed his or her life. At times, the contributor directly addresses those individuals facing similar challenges. In witnessing these respective journeys of recovery, hearing such words of empathy, the reader cannot help but be infused with courage, comfort, and optimism.

To the individuals whose stories grace this book, we extend our sincere appreciation and respect. You are very brave—not just for enduring the journey of recovery, but for sharing your experiences in hopes that others may benefit from your self-discoveries.

To the people who are reading these pages, we wish you continued strength, perseverance, and hope. Simply picking up this book indicates that you seek healing, that your world—while ravaged by an eating disorder—nurtures the courage and compassion that feeds recovery. In spirit, we stand by you. We honor and support your journey.

Jane Norstrom
Cindy Schallock
Shannon Simper
*Methodist Hospital*
*Eating Disorders Institute*

* *For privacy purposes, the names of those individuals who shared their stories have been changed.*

## The Journey

*One day you finally knew*
*what you had to do, and began,*
*though the voices around you*
*kept shouting*
*their bad advice—*
*though the whole house*
*began to tremble*
*and you felt the old tug*
*at your ankles.*
*"Mend my life!"*
*each voice cried.*
*But you didn't stop.*
*You knew what you had to do,*
*though the wind pried*
*with its stiff fingers*
*at the very foundations—*
*though their melancholy*
*was terrible.*
*It was already late*
*enough, and a wild night,*
*and the road full of fallen*
*branches and stones.*
*But little by little,*
*as you left their voices behind,*
*the stars began to burn*
*through the sheets of clouds,*
*and there was a new voice,*
*which you slowly*
*recognized as your own,*
*that kept you company*
*as you strode deeper and deeper*
*into the world,*
*determined to do*
*the only thing you could do—*
*determined to save*
*the only life you could save.*

—Mary Oliver
(from *Dream Work*)

*My own voice is back, telling me that I can accept myself for who I am. In the process of accepting myself, I have learned to give.*

*—Katie*

# Katie

I don't understand a lot of the details of my eating disorder in terms of how it started. I was always small physically, and I always had a voracious appetite. I swam three hours a day, and I just ate constantly, so I thought it was normal. But people started commenting on how much I could eat and how small I stayed. And I developed late; I got my period when I was fifteen. So as my body started changing, I began to think, "Maybe my appetite and food intake aren't normal; maybe I need to eat less." From there, things spiraled downward. My eating disorder began at the age of fifteen. But by the time I was seventeen, I was using it as a coping mechanism to deal with different losses, such as my grandpa dying and my sister going to school in Mexico.

I have always been a perfectionist—one of the traits that they say is stereotypical of someone who has anorexia—and I was incredibly sensitive. My feelings were easily hurt and I was always seeking to please people in any way I could. I really don't remember much about the four years when the eating disorder was such a huge part of my life because I was so much in my own world and couldn't come out. It had a big impact on my personality, on how I grew up in my teens, and on how I presented myself to others.

When I entered my senior year of high school, the only thing that was important to me was my eating disorder. I was depressed and attempted suicide a couple of times because of it. I dropped all my honors classes. I started swimming again in the fall, but then bulimia came into the picture, and I quit swimming. I had been captain of the swim team, so I still attended all the meets (at the urging of my coach). But I just didn't care. I didn't have the energy to care anymore because I was consumed by the eating disorder.

I started my treatment when I was fifteen—by seeing a therapist. When I was sixteen, I enrolled in an outpatient treatment program for eating disorders. I did this outpatient program until late fall of my junior year, when I quit because I told myself I was better and didn't need it anymore. I was admitted to the inpatient program at the age of seventeen, and I followed up with four weeks of partial hospitalization treatment at that same hospital. I continued the program over the summer and into the fall, then was in an outpatient program for about two months. At that point, I quit, having had enough of the program; I was just sick of it being such a big part of my life. I enrolled in yet another eating disorders treatment program the summer before my freshman year of college (at age eighteen). In college, I saw three or four different therapists, never staying with anyone long enough to really work things out with them. I pretty much felt that if things got rough, I could just leave or complain that the therapist was crappy so that I could switch treatment programs and start over and play all of these games.

Throughout all this time, I never admitted that I had an eating disorder. I always had this obscured perception about what was happening. "I am not as thin as most people," I thought, "and I don't have symptoms as severe as most people with eating disorders, so this is a waste of time. Just let me be. If I get bad, I'll come back." In inpatient treatment, I did have support and people—peers and nurses, primarily—to actually talk to, unlike in my house, where we didn't really ever talk about serious issues like this one. It was nice to know that people weren't going to give up on me.

During the early part of my treatment, I was honest only with a select few. My dietitian was one of them. For some reason, we just clicked personality-wise and I just dropped my guard with her. As far as therapy, though, my dishonesty definitely hindered my recovery. It wasn't that I lied so much as it was that I just didn't talk very much—

which, looking back, I regret, because those were the times when help was right there. The therapists were begging for me to let it out, and now I know that there is still stuff way down there that I really wish I could have processed and gotten rid of forever. I was not a pleasant patient at all. But I did love my dietitian and deep down, I know that I liked my therapist. I just wasn't going to let them know that.

I am thankful now for the times people put their foot down and pushed me to make it work instead of running from it. I am also grateful for the times when the treatment team did not listen to me—like when I would ask for a different meal plan—because it wasn't me wanting those things. It was the eating disorder. I cherish a quote by Corrie ten Boom: "When the train goes through a tunnel and the world gets dark, do you jump out? Of course not. You sit still and trust the engineer to get you through." My engineer is God, and he has certainly pulled me through!

My parents were incredibly supportive and did anything they could to help me, but they just didn't understand. I'm not sure you can be 100 percent supportive if you haven't been through an eating disorder yourself. I knew my mom and dad got sick of hearing mc talk about food, the incessant thoughts in my head, and how treatment was going, but at the time it felt like they didn't care. In reality, they just didn't know what to do or say. When they did show support, it never seemed right and I knew they were in a lose-lose situation, so they just avoided it as much as possible.

The hardest part about my parents not "getting it" was that they couldn't separate the eating disorder from me, and as a result, there was a lot of blaming, frustration, and anger. If I refused to drink 1 percent milk, for example, they would get mad and tell me to stop acting so stupid, then pour it for me and set the glass in front of me. That did not help. I wanted them to listen to how my head rationalized it. I wanted them to get mad at the disorder, show me why it might have been irrational, and validate that what I was thinking and feeling was real. I don't blame them, though, because I really believe they did all that they knew to do.

Despite the fact that both of my parents really didn't understand the eating disorder, I knew that they would be there if I needed them. I knew I could also count on my sister, even though she was thousands of miles away in Mexico (and, later, Asia).

I also had a best friend who was amazing. Honest to God, I couldn't have gotten through it without her. She knew, for instance, that I never would want to go out to eat with our friends, but she would call me and ask me to come anyway, and that invitation meant so much—like I wasn't falling off the face of the earth. She would say, "If you ever want to come back to us, I am here. You will always be part of the group." That helped a lot. And she was also doing the tougher things that a friend has to do. If I was not eating lunch, she would call me on it. Ultimately, whether I ate lunch or not was my decision, and she wouldn't get angry if I chose not to eat that meal, but she still stayed aware. A lot of my friends were into waiting for special times to have a one-on-one conversation with me, which was pretty confrontational and uncomfortable. ("Katie, we need to talk," they would say, and then begin drilling me with questions and concerns.) Other friends and even some teachers would treat the eating disorder as the elephant in the room—something that needs to be acknowledged but is avoided. But my best friend was different. She would say, "I'm noticing this, and if you want help, I will help you. But if you don't want help, that's fine. Let's just keep talking." It was perfect. So I think I really had a strong support network. I just didn't realize it at the time.

Another group of people that has played a huge role in my recovery is the family for which I nanny. I am now the godmother of a beautiful baby girl, and I have learned more from this child and her family than they will ever learn from me. I am filled with joy when I am with them—everything is simple, innocent, and literally sensible: Life is fun! Play hard! And love lots! To feel accepted as I am, to be loved and valued and looked up to, and to have someone or something else to invest my energy and heart into has been very healing. Finding a passion—getting and staying involved in life—somehow can help you keep your sanity, give you a place to find relief, and give you a way to hold on to who you are.

When my friend Andrea committed suicide as a result of her eating disorder, I turned a bit of a corner. It wasn't the corner to full recovery, but it was a step. I went to the funeral and grieved the loss of her. I didn't deal with grief well at that time, and so I went back to the eating disorder. But at one point, things did sink in, and I realized the true effect that an eating disorder can have on a person. I told myself, "I can't do this anymore. For Andrea alone, I cannot do this. I can't let her death be in vain by continuing to do this to myself. I want to do something with my life." I had attempted suicide exactly two months before Andrea did, and I was so angry at the world, wondering why

Andrea was taken and I wasn't. All this trying leads up to the vital moment at which you turn to God or another higher power and say, "You must do this." It was at this point that I began to get better. I gave up control and stopped trying, by my own effort, to heal myself. I simply was not strong enough.

Because of Andrea's death, I eventually changed my major to psychology. In putting my energy into education and prevention about eating disorders, I realized that I could not help anyone until I was completely recovered myself. And life got a lot more complicated and ugly as I began to face what I had always been running from. I was feeling really happy about my decision to get better, yet I was sad about my progress. I felt like my life was falling apart, but it was a good sign. In other words, I finally wanted to get well but was upset with myself for not being able to do it quickly or perfectly, as I had expected I should. That awareness was a positive. I was able to feel these emotions and not shove them away. It was a good time for me to be in treatment. I started actually working to get better, and it paid off. By my sophomore year of college, I had a good foundation under me. I stopped seeing things through the eyes of the eating disorder and began to see the world as it really was—a beautiful place.

I often wish I was one of those people who could say, "I am going to recover, starting now!" and then recover. But it was not so smooth for me, and I don't expect it is for the majority of people struggling with such intense and complicated disorders. Even during my recovery period, there was a lot of back-and-forth between wanting to keep the eating disorder in my life and wanting to get better. When I'd have lapses, my parents would say, "What are you doing to yourself? Have you forgotten about Andrea?" The constant swinging was hard on them—and me. I felt, at times, like I was losing my mind. I felt as if every time I made a decision or thought I figured something out, it would change. As I understand it now, I could not distinguish between myself and my eating disorder, and that impeded my recovery completely. In order for a person to outlive an eating disorder and see the true self, he or she has to see what the eating disorder is. A person who is trying to be free from an eating disorder needs to know what will be there when the eating disorder is released. The energy invested in self-blame must be transferred entirely to fighting the disorder.

You don't go into treatment and get better in one week or two weeks. You have to be patient and realize that even when you are fully recovered from the eating disorder, there will be some hard times. If you expect that these hard days will come, you can prepare for them, and they won't catch you off-guard. Rather than regard the tough times as a total relapse, you can see them as a natural part of the recovery process, which is often how I regarded my situation when I decided to fight the eating disorder while still holding myself to the expectation that I had to be perfect.

Recently my sister got married, and before the wedding, my whole family went on a diet. It wasn't necessarily a negative thing for them. I wanted to diet too, but for me personally, with my history of eating disorders, I would have had a hard time with it. I knew that I could not lose weight and exercise all the time because I would slide out of control. I know that about myself, which is good. My mom had said to me, "If you want to lose ten pounds, go ahead. You can do it; just do it safely." She is completely clueless to the fact that there is no safe way for me to diet right now. Hopefully, some day I will be able to lose five pounds if I want to or just get healthy and exercise a little more without being compulsive. But right now, I can't.

I feel like I am recovered, but I do not know what really defines recovery. I still struggle sometimes; it always seems like such a slippery slope. But every time I am tempted to go back to my eating disorder, I realize how close I am coming to truly helping other people. There's a great quote by former major league baseball coach Gene Mauch: "You can't lead anyone else further than you have gone yourself." Its message motivates me and grounds me in the reality that I have come a long way, that I have not journeyed alone, and that I have much more to see and do—both for myself and others. The fact that I am not perfect might be one of the most beautiful things about me.

Now that I am better, my relationships are so amazing. I am so much happier. I feel more freedom. If I don't exercise, it's okay. If I go on a vacation for a few days and eat nothing but greasy foods, it's okay. And my perspective has changed in terms of what I think about. I am beyond just thinking about my own little world, the world that was the eating disorder. I see now that other people have feelings and serious issues and problems. It's a wonderful feeling to be able to listen to them and really care. It's not that I did not care at all before, but now I have a strong compassion. I take great joy in helping people. And I enjoy life. When I am walking or running now, I see the sunset and the trees and the sky. I hear the birds singing, people laughing. It's not just about burning calories anymore. I also have a taste for music and movies and books, which I didn't in high school, because all I cared about was the eating disorder.

I have gained a lot as a result of having an eating disorder. I feel like I am so much more in tune with myself and other people because of what I have gone through. I have had to search myself, dig in, and really gain insight and understanding. Sir Edmund Hillary said, "It is not the mountain we conquer but ourselves." Having reached the summit of my own emotional mountain, I realize how true this statement is!

To the people who are going through an eating disorder, I would say, "Trust the people who are trying to help you. And trust yourself, too." Getting better can be scary. Even when you choose recovery, it's one of the hardest things in the world. It means letting go of what you think is control, and you don't know if you will fall. You don't know if you are going to go insane or get fat or never stop eating; these are all things that I was afraid of. But none of them happened. The therapy treatment team will catch you if they see you falling. They are there to make sure you don't eat too much or get sick or hurt yourself. But you have to trust them. You have to try. Watch for the little triumphs—like going to a movie with friends and enjoying it, or eating a piece of cake and realizing that it did not make you gain two pounds.

For parents and support persons of those with eating disorders, I would suggest reading up on the disorder and listening to your child or family member or friend. Try to understand or see it from your loved one's perspective. It is surprising how something seemingly absurd can become more understandable when you step inside another person's mind for a minute.

I look back at my high school years and wish I had done so many things differently, and I hate that. I don't ever want to have any more regrets about my life. Now I work really hard to make sure that I don't go back to the eating disorder. I want to use my energy to help others and to live life as it was meant to be lived. My own voice is back, telling me that I can accept myself for who I am.

In the process of accepting myself, I have learned to give. I have a passion for working with people who have eating disorders. I have been involved in starting a peer-counseling program on my college campus, making educational presentations, organizing support groups for students, and working on awareness campaigns to educate teachers, students, and parents about eating disorders. It has been great to help those who have gone through what I have. I have a heart for it, and I feel like that's a blessing.

*Katie is now twenty-two years old and has graduated from college with an undergraduate degree in psychology. She is currently applying for graduate schools, specifically doctorate programs in clinical psychology. She hopes one day to work professionally in the field of eating disorders treatment and research.*

## *Entries from Katie's journal*

*The following passages are journal entries that Katie has written within the past several years. Viewed collectively, her thoughts encapsulate the spectrum of emotions along the path of recovery—the frustration in not being understood, the denial of an illness, the gradual awareness that healing is paramount, the self-discovery, and finally, the courage, self-confidence, and wisdom that comes from overcoming an eating disorder.*

*Throughout her entries, Katie incorporates what is known as the language of narrative therapy. Narrative therapy is a psychological therapy approach that centers on people as the experts in their own lives. As it applies to treatment of eating disorders, narrative therapy uses respectful, non-blaming language to separate the eating disorder from the person. By using narrative language, people can move problems from within themselves to a new place outside their own identity. For example, instead of saying, "I am out of control because of my eating disorder," a person using narrative language might say, "The voice of the eating disorder is very strong today."*

***Junior year in high school, the summer after inpatient hospitalization:***

There's so much in my head, so much playing into [the disease] that it's hard to understand. Why can't I just recover? The biggest thing of all, though, is that I'm just so afraid… afraid that if I don't maintain strict control over my eating and exercise, I'll lose control completely and get fat. I fear being fat more than anything—and not because other people won't love me anymore because I know that's not true. No one cares what I look like! It's just that I can't stand to live in my skin when it is so disgusting and huge!!! I hate it! I'm scared that my hunger will never be satisfied by a moderate amount of food and if I won't be satisfied, why eat at all?

I also fear that if I give up this "obsession," which I'll readily admit that it has become, my protection will be taken away. If the eating disorder were gone, I would have to accept responsibility for my faults, my mistakes. There would be nothing to hide behind, nothing to blame for my imperfection. I'm an incredibly bad person at the core and could never take responsibility for it all; it would just simply be too much.

***Freshman year in college:***
Maybe the problem isn't just my inability to accept that I am not a bad person, but also my inability to accept that maybe I am actually a good person. I am realizing only now that while denying my weaknesses this whole time, I have also been denying my strengths. The same lies telling me that I wasn't good enough "as is," that I needed to hide my real self from others, also convinced me that I was unworthy or undeserving of praise. No wonder I can't see all of the good things about me that I know must be there! The eating disorder has convinced me that they don't exist.

***From this year:***
People keep asking how I did it, what changed, what the answer is to this insidious disease. It's so hard to know. I was living in it. It was part of me and I couldn't see the distinction. I want so much to understand what happened so that I can offer hope to people who think it'll never end, like I once did…

***A few weeks after the above entry:***
I found a quote from Albert Einstein and it's got me thinking: "Insanity: doing the same things over and over and expecting different results." I think I began to recover when I saw that this was true—that I kept doing the same things over and over again, expecting that "this time, it will be different."

I have realized that recovery is hard! VERY HARD! Probably one of the hardest things I will ever have to do in my life!

I have learned to expect and accept lapses, knowing that after six years of living according to the eating disorder, it would most likely creep up from time to time—and that it's okay. MaryEllen [Clausen, founder of Ophelia's Place in Syracuse, New York and mother of two daughters who struggled with severe anorexia] uses this saying that I love: "All I want is for you to struggle honestly." And that is what I long to do—just to be real with it. No more secrets, no lying or making things worse than they really are in my mind. I will just face it as it is, whether it is good or bad. I will struggle honestly because I know that's what the eating disorder does not want. I think this is huge for other people to know about—that it's okay to struggle and that there is freedom in being honest about it.

I am still tempted today sometimes; certain situations, people, or moods make me an easy target for the eating disorder's lies. But I have come to expect them and know that I cannot drop my guard. I've fallen and I've given in even this past year, but that just has to be okay. You are not perfect—deal with it, Katie! When I am discouraged that my eating disorder is not completely gone, I try to remember where I have come from and all that I have accomplished.

Remembering how incredibly lost I was, how much pain I was in, and how strongly the eating disorder had control of my mind and body allows me to see the strength humans have inside of them. I am a researcher and I know that the statistics don't always agree, but I refuse to believe that ANYONE is too far gone in the grips of this disease to reach full recovery. If we get ANGRY, if we hold each other accountable, if we fight harder when the eating disorder screams louder, if we forgive ourselves for falling, and most importantly, if we hold onto hope, we can come out on the other side of this disease and live happy and productive lives! That is exciting! It fuels what I do and I feel strangely honored to have shared in the struggles so many women and men face. To have been on the inside and to now see it from the outside is truly a gift. I have been changed forever and am not sure I would change things if I could go back. All things happen for a reason, and I'm slowly beginning to understand the reasoning behind the last six years of my life!

*Everything will be all right in the end.*
*If it's not all right, then it isn't the end.*

—*Author Unknown*

*With the eating disorder, I'd walk into a room*
*and be carrying death on my arm...*
*Now, that constant haunting has left me.*

*—Molly*

# Molly

As is probably the case with other young people, the eating disorder in my life did not happen overnight. It began as an awareness of food, a worrying about my body size. By the middle of high school, the eating disorder became the focus of my life.

During the period when the eating disorder—primarily anorexia—began, I was in tenth grade. I was playing competitive tennis and also doing tae kwon do, a sport in which "weighing in" was important for matches. I was struggling with depression and some family instability. My parents were divorced, and my brother had moved out of the house, then moved back in, then left again. Things were not perfect. I was feeling very isolated, and as the eating disorder advanced, my isolation deepened. But from the outside, to my friends and teachers in high school, no one would have thought anything was really wrong. I was a good student. I was participating in sports.

The feelings of isolation became more pronounced as I moved to the East Coast, where I enrolled in the Rhode Island School of Design. I was alone, but because I seemed to be totally functional—getting good grades, attending classes—everyone assumed I was healthy.

The summer before my junior year in college, I was living back at home in Minnesota. By this time, my eating disorder had reached a level of severity that made it difficult to conceal. I was scheduled to leave for Rome at the end of the summer to study art and architecture for the entire school year. But I was not concentrating on learning or experiencing the culture. I was too busy working on my eating disorder in complete solitude. Going to Rome, I thought, would get me out of the country. I could be as sick as I wanted to be. I was looking forward to being really ill all by myself in Italy. All of a sudden, I became scared. I realized that I had a problem. I had this strong sense of fatality—this strong feeling that if I went to Italy, I would die. The eating disorder would take my life.

When I realized this, I went to my mom. "I have an eating disorder," I told her, "and I need help." She called the hospital that afternoon and the eating disorders treatment center there said, "Oh, we have a long waiting list." But my mother would just not take "no" for an answer.

"You just have to get her in," she kept saying. And within a few hours, they called back and said that they had an opening. They said that I could come in three days.

Once I revealed that I had an eating disorder, my family was incredibly responsive. My parents had known other parents whose children had struggled with an eating disorder. They were aware that it existed, and they knew enough about it to know that treatment was available. They took it seriously right away. An outpatient program proved to be the best option for me because I lived near the hospital and because my family was so supportive and able to provide 24-hour care.

There are two reasons why treatment really worked for me. The first reason is because I chose to go treatment. I met so many people—in treatment and elsewhere—who were forced into treatment by family and friends, and a lot of those people didn't recover because they didn't see they had a problem. So the first key to having successful treatment is to want to be there in the first place—and to know that you have a problem that needs to be addressed.

The second reason that my treatment was successful was because of the phenomenal way that my treatment program was set up. I had a nurse, doctor, therapist, and dietitian, and I received both individual and group therapy. It was so balanced, and all of my needs were met. I was at treatment practically every day, so it was intense. But I think the arrangement was pretty ideal.

This is not to say that recovery was easy. When you're in treatment, you wade through and eventually navigate your own psychology as to how you arrived where you are in life, and it's complicated to be honest with yourself right away. So in the beginning of treatment, much of it was about hiding and concealing and being elusive about both food and my feelings. The biggest challenge was trying to change my whole way of thinking, my code of behaviors. I had all of these illogical rules and systems in my mind that had to do with food. I was dividing food into an arbitrary system of "solids" and "liquids." Solids were to be avoided, while liquids were okay. It was not logical at all, and it was a lot of work to break those rules down to determine how valid they were. My dietitian was very patient with me in discussing whether the rules I imposed were grounded in reality.

Sometimes when people are sick, they have a tendency to romanticize illness. I was one of those people. I was training to be a professional artist and painter, and like some others who are creative, I had a tendency to romanticize the suffering. In treatment, there was a lot of discussion about leading a life that was more balanced, a life in moderation, which can go a little bit against the artistic spirit when you are caught up in creativity. When you are an artist, it's not about being balanced; it's often about *not* being moderate—doing things like staying up, never sleeping. It took me some time, but eventually I realized that being sick with an eating disorder was not helping me to be an artist.

I did not go to Italy right away. In my junior year, I transferred to a college in my hometown for that fall semester and continued treatment. When the second semester began, I went back to Rhode Island, where I continued to be involved in a comprehensive treatment program. Then during the summer break, I came back home and continued the treatment I was in the summer before. All along the way to recovery, I had relapses and slips. Over time, they became less and less frequent—something like how it might be for smokers who quit and have the occasional cigarette until finally, they are no longer smoking.

The signs of recovery were easy to see; some were immediate, some weren't, but they were all rewarding. I was starting to eat, and therefore sleep, which made me feel better physically. In time, I was able to go out to lunch and realize that I didn't have to be completely worried about food and could actually enjoy being out to lunch with a friend. I could go for a walk and not feel dizzy; I could enjoy the outdoors again. My work as an artist returned, and it was even better than when I was sick. In the process of re-nourishing my body, small payoffs of recovery were showing themselves.

In my senior year in college, I made the trip to Italy. I do admit that I struggled there a bit. My friends were alert to the eating disorder and aware that things weren't going well at first, and they contacted my parents. My parents just straightforwardly said that I had to get help if I was struggling—and that if I didn't, I'd have to come back home. I got connected with an Italian psychotherapist who was trained in London, and she was wonderful. So I relapsed initially, but I got back on track quickly. I finished my senior year in Italy and then stayed there to work as an artist for another two years.

In terms of support, I would have to say that my parents—my mother and stepfather—were the primary people participating in the therapy with me. They let me do the work I needed to do to heal. They were always there and ready to help, but they also gave me the space to really recover, and that was important, because recovery is such a private process. Sometimes, even the most well-intentioned supporters are too involved, too overbearing, and that ends up putting a lot of pressure on the person trying to recover. I can't honestly think of anything that I would have wanted them to do differently in the recovery process. They were very receptive to the cues and directions they received from the clinicians during my treatment.

My friends and other family members also stayed by my side. Some of my relationships even became stronger. When my best friend from college heard that I was sick, he flew out during the semester and visited me. Everyone—my professors, fellow classmates, friends, family—were shocked when they learned I was having a problem. Many of them asked, "How could we not have known? How could we not have seen this?" And they felt guilty. But the treatment team kept saying, "Let's just focus on the recovery." They knew that there was the tendency for family and friends to have feelings of guilt and blame, but they also knew that those feelings were not going to aid in the recovery process.

When I came back from Europe—at about age twenty-four—I enrolled in graduate school at the University of Minnesota. Since being back here, I have been seeing a therapist on and off as a monthly "touching base"—an extension of my recovery. One thing that I discovered, based on lots of testing, is that I have many of the symptoms characteristic of obsessive-compulsive disorder. So I have learned perhaps that what has happened to me may not have been all eating disorder. It could have just been how I was wired.

Today, my life is completely different. With the eating disorder, I'd walk into a room and be carrying death on my arm. There was always this physical presence hovering over me, dragging me down. Now, that constant haunting has left me. It is hard for me to imagine that I even once had an eating disorder; it is that far away. In the course of telling the story of my eating disorder, I have a hard time remembering some of the early events because they seem so separate from my life today. And while I wouldn't have wanted to have an eating disorder, I know that I would not want to change my history, because through treatment and the people I have gotten to know, I have received many gifts.

But I lost, too. I lost time with my family and friends, many hours when I was not present with them—or myself.

The hardest thing for people with an eating disorder to realize is that they can be completely better. I can't tell you how I know that to be true, but I can say that my recovery is an example. At the time you are entering therapy, it seems unattainable, but if you just do the daily steps of treatment, you will be getting closer to recovery. Don't take on too much during your treatment. Keep it simple. Don't think about the big picture. Take it one step at a time, one meal at a time. It was helpful to me to be told that I did not have to be thinking about what was going to happen down the road. I just had to focus on getting through lunch.

*Molly is now twenty-eight years old. She recently received a master of fine arts and master of arts degree in art history from the University of Minnesota. She is currently teaching high school and college students. Molly's art work has received the attention of art collectors and galleries. She is making plans to show her work at a well-known metropolitan art gallery.*

*There are no shortcuts to*
*any place worth going.*

*—Beverly Sills*

*My family and I are more open with one another now. I have gained an appreciation for families that feel strong enough to accept their faults and deal with them—rather than to pretend everything is normal when clearly it's not.*

*—Sarah*

# Sarah

Officially, the eating disorder began when I was fifteen years old—or at least that was when the diagnosis was made. In reflection, the eating disorder was actually in the works since I was eight. Thoughts of it started when I was in third grade.

When the eating disorder began, the most significant things happening were changes in my appearance. I was in dance class and I think that played a role. Things in our family were somewhat chaotic. My dad was working a lot, trying to get a business off the ground. My mom had recently returned to work. I looked much older than I actually was and therefore had older boys saying things to me that made me feel uncomfortable. I recall specifically that I was getting intensely perfectionistic at that time and expecting a lot from myself with schoolwork. I questioned myself for the first time in my life. I felt ugly and uncoordinated, and I started worrying about how I looked in my ballet leotard. I started worrying about friends—whether I was liked, whether I fit in. I started worrying about my parents and my siblings. I remember worrying about food and becoming more picky with it and seeing how it affected me. And I remember noting the feeling of fullness and not liking it. I recall not wanting to eat very much and liking the feeling of hunger.

I do not think the eating disorder had much of an effect on my life in its early stages. I think it slowed, then progressed, and at times turned off. I remember most vividly the eating disorder thoughts getting strong when I was thirteen years old. At that time, I was entering junior high school. We had moved to another part of town and so I needed to make new friends, and I was extremely nervous about that. I recall being considered attractive, but I definitely did not see myself that way. The focus on boys at that time was very strong and I was really scared about it. The part of my life that stands out most at that time was the constant evaluation. Your peers evaluate you. The teachers are evaluating you as a student. Every athletic team you participated in had tryouts, and consequently, you were placed on an "A" or "B" team. I wanted to be involved, so I tried out for everything. But I panicked about everything and went into it all believing I wasn't good enough. At that time, the association between my weight and "being good enough" was solidified. I began to focus on my appearance whenever I had times of uncertainty and evaluation. By the end of junior high, I was continually focusing on healthy foods. In fact, I recall a specific instance in home economics class when we evaluated our food for a day, and I was obsessed with having the least amount of fats and the most fruits and vegetables in the class—just to get the praise of the teacher. I remember not eating before attending social and athletic events. By the time I completed ninth grade, I had experimented with purging and felt satisfaction in it.

***

When I was sixteen, I got scared by how incredibly strong the thoughts became. One night, I became so overwhelmed by them that I confided in my mom that I was struggling with eating disorder behavior. Instantly, my family went out and got me to see a therapist, and I was admitted to an inpatient psychiatry program shortly thereafter. I sat in my room that first night, crying hysterically and begging my parents to discharge me. I believed I could stop the thoughts and behaviors if they took me out of the hospital. They also wanted to believe, and I was discharged despite the advice of the clinicians. Meanwhile, everyone at school had found out, and I was really embarrassed. I was determined not to keep the attention on me, and I challenged myself to stop the behaviors. What I found instead was that the eating disorder was flourishing. I think the eating disorder had me believing that I was not thin enough and that therefore, I had received an unjust diagnosis. The eating disorder continued to spiral out of control, and in my senior year of high school, I was again admitted to an inpatient program. This time, the admission was much longer, and for the first time, I accepted and believed I had an eating disorder and needed treatment for it. On the downside, the only reason I believed I needed help was because of the depression that kicked in. One night, while driving home, I had the thought of driving my car into a telephone pole; I was just so tired. That was when I told my mom I needed help. In my heart, though, I thought the main reason I needed help was due to the depression, and throughout the treatment, I believed if I could "balance" the eating disorder and keep my moods up, I would be fine.

In some ways I was honest with the treatment team—at least as honest as I could've been at that point. I think there were some moments of really challenging therapy sessions in which I was facing a lot of difficult issues. But when something difficult arises and when the eating disorder is your only coping mechanism, the thoughts and behaviors of the eating disorder roar. One thing I discovered during treatment was how anorexia and bulimia played off of one another. I also realized how I saw the anorexia as the "okay" eating disorder and the bulimia as the wrong eating disorder that needed "fixing."

***

I certainly had the utmost support from my family. Granted, they were in the dark most of the time as far as what was the right way to respond to things going on with me, as they had never experienced loved ones doing the things to themselves that I was. At this point, I do not feel I can say that anything they did was helpful or not helpful, because I do not want to place any blame. I can say that all families will inevitably say and do things that the person with the eating disorder will say is *not* helpful. Everyone will make comments on the food/weight/exercise, but it's a natural response because the eating disorder sends an entire family spinning. The eating disorder will get everyone feeling crazy and will get people suffering with it to believe everyone is out to get them—meaning that when a person is in the midst of an eating disorder, he or she will think everyone is focused on helping them to "get fat." The person with the eating disorder will say and do so many hurtful things to loved ones, and it is only human for family members to react with their own set of feelings. Looking back, I see now that this exchange of emotions was part of the process. That said, the most helpful thing to me seems to have been when I got to a certain age and stage in my recovery when my family could "let go." Suddenly, they could listen to me talk about therapy and my own self-realizations—without trying to fix the problem.

***

Early on, the challenges of treatment involved getting a therapist I connected with. I also found that, as an adolescent, it was difficult feeling as though nothing was confidential. I felt whatever I said in treatment could've gone to my parents, and I know that these perceptions affected my honesty with the treatment team. In regard to becoming my own individual, I encountered some difficult situations because at times I was not ready to challenge my parents; I merely wanted to discuss thoughts I had that differed from theirs. I desperately wanted my independence. I desperately wanted to find out who I was. I think that these feelings were typical of a teenager, yet it was hard for me to find the compromise between being the "perfect" daughter, friend, student, and athlete and trying new things to discover my own identity.

After high school graduation, I left home, and this is when I saw everything changing. My parents connected me immediately with a therapist, whom I ended up working with for seven years. It was through that therapeutic relationship that I eventually found recovery. She had a strict policy of seeing only the patient. At no time would she even meet my family members. To me, that opened the door to being honest with her. It also signified to me that it didn't matter what the "truth" was of what I told; the only important issue was my perspective, and we worked with that. That approach differed so much from earlier therapy, in which I would talk to my therapist about something and then my parents and I would talk about it in another session and it became a debate over who was "right." With my new therapist, if I thought my mother had said something hurtful, for example, we would deal with the fact that I perceived what she said as hurtful. That approach was key for me. I realized I would analyze what people said and did and really obsess about it. While working with this therapist, I would evaluate what I heard people say to me and why I thought as I did about what people said. It didn't matter if the person said what I thought; it was the fact that I heard them in a certain way and obsessed about it and that it affected my life and the eating disorder. Because of this type of approach, I also found my therapist to be my support person. What was important was for me to see and deal with my reality.

As far as slips and relapses, I had plenty. Whenever I would take one step forward, it seemed that the eating disorder would reshape itself and I would find myself three steps back. I would say the worst the eating disorder ever got was from the ages of eighteen to twenty-three. Between the fasting, excessive exercising, and bingeing and purging, I was 100 percent caught up in it. I almost failed out of college. In fact, I look back at college as a miserable experience. I jeopardized my safety every day. I would be in the Twin Cities leaving the dorms or my apartment at all hours of the night. I would go exercise in the middle of the night. I knew every single bathroom in restaurants, on campus, in hotels, gas stations, and malls—and when they were accessible. I would drive for great distances to go to restaurants where I wouldn't see people from school and then drive to restrooms to purge. I knew when the maintenance people at school cleaned certain bathrooms at night and I knew which ones I could access on campus. All of my integrity was compromised. But I got to the point where I didn't care if people knew what I was doing. I was operating on the sheer fear of needing to purge. My freshman year in college, I went home for a funeral and returned to my dorm room to find my roommates had moved out. My sophomore year, I lived off campus and almost destroyed my relationship with my roommates, all of whom were exceptional women. I lived on my own my junior year, and the eating disorder loved that. I worked jobs just to support the eating disorder. The eating disorder thrived on my anonymity. I did nothing socially because the thought of going out in public was too overwhelming for me. I lost at least one grade point in every single class I took because of absences.

Through it all, however, tiny steps of recovery were occurring. I worked with my therapist, and she stuck by me for all of those years. I recall the first time I went to dinner with my sister and as usual, I planned to purge. But something happened. We were having so much fun talking that I found myself sitting there at the table a few hours after eating, and it felt as though I could manage to get through a meal without purging. Another time I went to dinner with friends, and rather than cancel out immediately, I challenged myself to hang out with them into the evening. I ended up having a great time. Granted, these were moments of extreme anxiety, but they were moments of triumph over the eating disorder. It was each and every one of these tiny moments that came together—and got me to the point of recovery.

***

Every day when I woke up while in college, I told myself, "Today is the last day I will have this eating disorder." Likewise, I went to bed every night praying that I would get some help from a greater power in dealing with it. So I didn't really have just one "aha" moment. One that stands out for me was in the winter of my freshman year. I had had a really bad eating disorder day. I started driving around the Twin Cities in the middle of the night, crying and pondering suicide. I realized during that evening that I did not want to die but that I wanted the eating disorder to die. I eventually found myself in an emergency room to see the on-call psychiatrist. Following that evening, I knew I wanted recovery.

Another time, I hit a low. I ended up finding my therapist's e-mail address and wrote her a long note, exposing everything I had not been 100 percent truthful about. At that moment, it dawned on me that I had not had a day in four years in which I didn't purge at least three times. That gave me a starting goal to work with. It also forced me to be more truthful with my therapist because I had to face her—embarrassed and scared—the following week.

***

At this point in my life, I cannot nail down a specific recovery point. In fact, I can only really say it feels accidental. Granted, throughout the years, I tried different strategies to fight the urges. I wrote in my journal. I took a semester off from college and worked with my therapist in an intensive outpatient setting. One identifiable strategy that I remember using was that each time I slipped, I stopped beating myself up over it. The eating disorder had me thinking in black-and-white terms. For instance, if I purged in the morning, the entire day was lost and there seemed no reason to fight against it. To recover, I needed to change that. So even though I might slip in the morning, I had to "get back on the horse" and keep fighting throughout the day. Another thing I did at one point was to write down what personality traits I thought I possessed within the bulimia and which ones I possessed within the anorexia. That was a huge step for me, as the eating disorder made me think I was going to lose those traits if I lost the eating disorder. For example, I really liked the spontaneity that I saw as part of the bulimia (and me). I also liked the goal-oriented part of the anorexia (and me). Once I wrote out all of the characteristics of each eating disorder, I started a list and a mind-set of being able to shape the (recovered) person I wanted to become. I got to pick and choose which personality traits I wanted the new "me" to possess. I allowed myself to explore ways to pull positive traits out of the bulimia/anorexia (which currently was the only way I identified myself) and move them into my new identity. It was beneficial for me to see how the two disorders played off one another.

Another thing that really worked for me was setting small personal challenges—for example, trying to not work out for a day and seeing how it affected me. I would establish "delays" after meals—for example, making myself wait ten minutes after eating before purging. Over time, the delays got longer, and I would find at times that the urge would wear off. I also found that during the delays, I enjoyed myself; rather than spending the half-hour after the meal obsessing about the "wheres" and "hows" of purging, I engaged in conversations with people I was with. I began trying new clothing options. I started buying clothes with elastic waist bands. That way, the clothes were more comfortable after I ate and thus did not foster the eating disorder thoughts as much. I found at times that I would accidentally oversleep and miss my morning workout—and that turned out to be okay. I found that without planning, over time, I enjoyed some activities I hadn't been able to for so long because of the eating disorder. For example, I went on a trip and found myself wearing a bikini for the first time in about ten years, and I felt okay in it. I started forcing myself not to hide behind the eating disorder. When I stopped hiding behind it, the positive reinforcements affected my self-esteem, which affected my ability to heal. Over time, I achieved recovery.

To anyone who has a loved one with an eating disorder, I would recommend seeing a professional about it so that you can talk to someone about the emotions you are experiencing. It is my perception that typically, in most families in which an eating disorder erupts, there may be other issues that other family members need to deal with. I look back and think of my siblings and how the eating disorder affected them and wish they had had someone to discuss things with.

***

Today, I am happy. I am free from the hell I found myself living in when I struggled with the eating disorder. I am real. I have had to learn to face and accept my less-than-desirable personality traits and be okay with them. I have also created balance in my life. I am married. I have a nice job. I still have eating disorder thoughts, but I have learned to identify them, and I have plenty of skills for coping with them. I think I will always have those thoughts, especially in stressful situations. But the voice is soft-spoken now. I would say 10 percent of my day has a focus on weight, appearance, food, and exercise. The other 90 percent is focused on life. I know now I am susceptible to the lure of the eating disorder, and I remind myself of that continuously. I am honest with those around me. My husband and family are aware of my challenges and can tell when I am obsessing about things, not just body image or weight but about about how I perceive interactions with people—comments people make that I may perceive as critical. My loved ones are there when the body image issues seem to be gaining an upper hand. When I have struggles today, they mostly revolve around thoughts about my body image. But now I have awareness of why my body image may be poorer on some days than others. I have strategies for addressing those thoughts. I catch myself if I am getting drawn into restrictive eating or excessive exercising and then force myself to get back on track.

I have a wonderful husband with whom I want to be an active participant in a relationship. I want to have children. I want to do well in my job. I want to maintain friendships. I want to continue having a healthy relationship with my family. All of these reasons help me fight the eating disorder. I used to tell myself that I needed to try life without the eating disorder and could go back to it if I found the eating disorder's way of life was better. I have not gone back. I do not think I will ever choose going back. Life is too good without it.

I definitely gained a lot through having an eating disorder. It gave me the opportunity to access therapy and become more introspective. Both myself and my family benefited from that. We are more open with one another now. I have gained an appreciation for families that feel strong enough to accept their faults and deal with them—rather than to pretend everything is normal when clearly it's not. I have gained an appreciation for people and the difficulties they may find themselves in.

*Sarah is now twenty-eight years old. She is married and working at a health care facility in the Midwest.*

*Always be a first-rate version of yourself,*
*instead of a second-rate version of someone else.*

*—Judy Garland*

*If someone would've told me...what I would go through during my senior year of high school, I would've thought they were crazy. But now that I look back on it, I think that in a way, I needed to go through it—in order to mature as a person, grow spiritually, and gain common sense.*

*—Chad*

# Chad

In the summer before my senior year of high school, I was training for my last season of cross-country running. I had been in the sport since seventh grade and was a dedicated runner. It was to be my last year of cross-country in high school, so I wanted to make sure I didn't waste my last chance. Therefore, I trained extra-hard; by that, I mean I tried to lose weight in order to run faster. Back then, I would describe myself as extremely serious and dedicated. There was never a training day where I didn't run. It was in this atmosphere that my eating disorder surfaced.

My eating disorder began with my trying to eat "healthy" foods, a practice that stemmed primarily from my running and active lifestyle. I stopped eating many desserts and fats. However, things soon snowballed, and in time, I was not eating any desserts or fats at all. I also began eating less and less because I kept thinking that if I were thin, I would run faster. Another part of my disordered behavior was being overly active. This included lifting weights, running excessively fast and far, and always taking the longer, harder route with just about anything. If I were going up the stairs, I would try to figure out a way to go up two or three times in order to burn the most calories possible. This behavior worsened as time went on.

In the early stages, the eating disorder had a huge effect on my life. I lost a lot of my carefree attitude, which I was known for among my relatives and friends. I stopped joking around and just enjoying life. I also lost my relationships with family members and friends. I stopped going out, I obsessed about food all the time, I felt guilty a lot of the time, and I had no energy to do anything. I realized that I wasn't having fun on my runs; I just got them over with. Because of the eating disorder, I didn't enjoy running anymore; I just did it like I was going to work every day.

I didn't seek treatment until December of my senior year. Even then, I wasn't the one who set up the appointments and sought out resources for treatment. Thankfully, my mother was able to assist me in making these decisions and taking these actions.

At first, I only had a psychologist. What helped was being able to talk to someone who would listen to what I was going through—and to have him or her know that I wasn't the reason for the eating disorder. Still, initially, I was skeptical in treatment; I thought people who went to psychologists were either lonely or lacked confidence. "Who needs someone to tell them how they should think?" I asked myself. "Why can't people just figure things out on their own?" I soon realized how helpful this type of treatment can be. I went to the psychologist three times in December. During this time, I also saw a nutritionist at a local hospital. In January, I was admitted to an inpatient program for people with eating disorders.

I was able to be honest with my treatment team, even in the beginning, when my parents were in the room and they found out for the first time what I had been doing and going through on a daily basis. At first, it was difficult for both them and me, but it was what had to be done for me to get better. Within three weeks, I was released from the inpatient program, at which time I began a month of outpatient treatment. After outpatient, I had checkups every two weeks or so, but gradually, they tapered off—until one day, the doctors told me I didn't need to come any more. I continued treatment with my psychologist through the summer after my senior year in high school.

I was extremely lucky and fortunate to have an excellent support network. I have parents, other relatives, friends, teachers, and community members who care about me and support me no matter what I am thinking or experiencing. Whether it was urging me to get treatment, being empathetic enough to care about my situation or just sitting down and listening to what I had to say, their interactions and connections with me during me treatment helped enormously. They were all the reason I got better as quickly as I did.

One of the best things that my loved ones and friends did is listen to my cares and concerns. I knew what I was doing to my body was terrible and unhealthy, but in the stage I was at, I couldn't force myself to act otherwise when it came to eating. Just telling me that they were thinking about me or praying for me was very helpful. The one thing that didn't help was when they tried to get me to eat by forcing me to eat something I didn't want to or asked why I just couldn't eat more. That's like asking a person with alcoholism why they can't stop drinking, like asking a person with arachnophobia why they can't just get along with spiders; it's just not that easy.

The biggest challenge in treatment was just learning to eat again. It meant being able to eat the right portions of food, eating foods I didn't feel comfortable eating, and not feeling guilty about eating. This was probably the most difficult phase of treatment. I had slips and relapses, particularly early on. They're inevitable and should not necessarily be construed as bad. I just learned from them and tried to overcome them the next time such a situation presented itself.

There were many reasons why I decided that I wanted to and could get well. Even though running was the ultimate reason for my eating disorder occurring, it was my first time running after being in the hospital that really pushed me to get better. I love running—and not for the caloric expenditure anymore. I love just being by myself—just being with the road and my thoughts. I knew that in order to get back to this solo activity, I had to eat, and so I made it my goal to get back as quickly as possible and be able to run in track that spring. Without this goal, I might have recovered, but I know the recovery wouldn't have been nearly as fast or successful as it was.

As I got well, I began restoring the relationships I had lost to the eating disorder over the previous six months. I became more carefree, I smiled more, and I spent more time with my friends. Most of all, I had so much free time not having to worry about what I was eating or how much I was eating. My voice had always been with me, but when I was healing, I learned to recognize what that voice was—and to listen to the positive things it was telling me.

I have changed in many ways since overcoming my eating disorder. I now know when to just let things go and accept them for how they are. I know when to keep pushing and when to say when. I know that I need food to be able to run, breathe, and live. However, I'm still the exuberant, optimistic teenager my parents always knew.

One of the things I am most happy to have restored after my encounter with eating disorders is my relationship with my parents, especially my mother. I know it hurt her terribly to see me drift away from her, emotionally and physically. So to finally be able to relate to each other like we used to is a blessing I will always be thankful for.

At first, I never told people the complete reason why I was in the hospital, but when I was ready, I began telling close friends and later, even entire sports teams at my school. Some were shocked, some cried, and some just accepted me as equal no matter what happened. You can never completely know how people will react to you, but you can always control how you act in their presence.

Today, the eating disorder is completely free from my life. I love just being able to eat whatever I want—within reason, of course—and not feel guilty about it. The only thing I sometimes think about is how far I have come in eighteen months. If someone would've told me the summer before what I would go through during my senior year of high school, I would've thought they were crazy. But now that I look back on it, I think that in a way, I needed to go through it—in order to mature as a person, grow spiritually, and gain common sense.

How did I know I was recovered? When I could eat anything and not feel guilty about it. I kept pushing myself to eat foods that were difficult for me, so when I crossed the last one off my list and had no problem with eating it, I knew I was almost fully recovered.

My advice for others dealing with eating disorders is to realize that it will not be easy. I have been a distance runner for seven years, and I can tell you that overcoming my eating disorder was possibly the most difficult thing I have ever had to do in my life. But it can be done and you can do it if you are willing to work at it a little every day. Realize that it will not happen overnight. It took me almost a year to overcome my eating disorder, and that was probably even faster than normal. But you can do it and you do have the ability.

For those supporting a person struggling with eating disorders, realize that it is no one's fault—neither yours nor your loved one's. The person you love who has the eating disorder probably wants to see the eating disorder go away just as much as you do, but that person needs help, and the best thing you can do is to offer support. Tell the person you love him or her, that you're there to help in any way possible, and that nothing will come between you both—an eating disorder or anything else. Above all, support and love this person unconditionally.

One of the things I lost because of my eating disorder was my absolute perfectionism and my obsessive thoughts about mundane things. What I have gained is a world of knowledge over the last eighteen months. I can't possibly begin to describe all that I have learned about my body, my thoughts, and myself. But I can say that I have emerged from this experience a better and changed person. I know the sky's the limit, and I'm setting my goals high from now on.

*Chad is now nineteen years old. He is a freshman in college and has successfully completed his first season of college cross-country. He can't wait for the second one.*

*Chad is still the terrific kid he always was;*
*he's just wiser and stronger.*

*—Audrey*

# Chad's Mom, Audrey

I noticed a marked difference in Chad's eating habits in July of 2002, the summer before his senior year in high school. He seemed to want to eat only fruits and vegetables, he drank a ton of water, and he became very choosy about eating foods with fat in them—pizza, chips, cookies. He denied that there was a problem, and he also became defensive when I questioned him.

I scheduled an appointment with our family doctor in the middle of September, but he was not concerned that Chad had lost seven pounds in two months. "He's a runner, and it's been a hot summer," he said. He agreed to do some blood work on Chad because I asked for it; I thought we should have the results for future reference, should something more develop in the months to come. (Little did I know!) I even scheduled an appointment for myself to talk with a family therapist to see if there was anything else I could do, but she said as long as the blood work came back okay, maybe there was no reason to do anything further.

Chad and I have always had an absolutely wonderful relationship; he would tell me anything and everything. By that fall, however, he was distancing himself from me and my husband, and he continued to be defensive. I remember one time he told me, "Mom, it seems like there's two of me. Part of me knows that what I'm doing isn't a good thing, and the other part can't do anything about it." Had I known then what I know now, I would have taken him in for treatment at that point. I think he felt absolutely powerless. I continued to be worried, but since the doctor wasn't concerned, and the therapist wasn't concerned, and his coach said, "It probably isn't an eating disorder, just disordered eating," I figured that perhaps I was making a mountain out of a molehill.

A doctor's appointment in late November didn't prove to be helpful, either. The weight check showed that Chad had not lost any additional weight (he admitted much later that he had drunk a lot of water before going to the appointment), so the doctor seemed to think things would be fine. When I asked about Chad's blue knuckles, the doctor chalked it up to dry skin and recommended some special hand lotions. By the end of the appointment, I was thinking, "Maybe I am crazy."

On Christmas Day, I asked my sister, who is a nurse, to talk with Chad. She took his hands, looked at his blue fingers and told him, "Chad, you could die from this." She had a serious talk with him, and on the way home, he cried as he admitted to not eating all of his school lunches, pacing back and forth in the lower hallway while we thought he was doing his homework, and not being able to focus in school. He also admitted that he needed help. So on the day after Christmas, I contacted an eating disorders treatment program administered through a nearby hospital. I took the first available appointment, which was January 14. From December 26 until his evaluation, Chad was at the local clinic every three or four days for electrocardiograms, blood work, and other laboratory work. And I absolutely made him eat everything I could; I was convinced that I had to get him to his appointment, and that once he was there, he would be in good hands. I was right.

It was frightening to be told at the evaluation that Chad had done damage to his heart to the point that he had to be immediately admitted to the inpatient program. My husband and I drove back to our home—45 miles from the hospital—to pick up his clothes and other belongings that he would need, while he stayed at the hospital. As I hugged him when we were leaving, I told him that he would have to work harder at his recovery than he'd ever worked before, and that, although this was something he was going to have to do himself, he wouldn't be alone; we would always be there for him. I also told him that there was a reason this was happening, although it might be a while before he could see that. It was horrible to have to leave him there.

Treatment was sometimes difficult for Chad. He didn't like not being able to be physically active. He was very down when he didn't make progress right away. He was testy at times, which is very unlike Chad. We visited every night and on every weekend, and others did as well—relatives, his best buddy and his parents, our pastor. But Chad didn't want everyone to know. He was embarrassed and afraid that others would make fun of him. Gradually, however, Chad grew stronger—physically, mentally, and emotionally. The staff in the inpatient and the partial hospitalization treatment programs were wonderful, and I can't begin to say enough about all they did for Chad and our family. They gave us our son back.

One of my frustrations during Chad's treatment was that almost all of the group therapy work was geared toward the female population. I completely understand why that is done (95 percent of patients with eating disorders are girls or women), but one of the things that was difficult for Chad to come to grips with was that he was a guy that was struggling, so it would have been nice if there had maybe been some attention paid to that.

As to expectations for the treatment, I was hoping that treatment would allow Chad at some point to go back to life as he knew it before the eating disorder. He was to be captain of the track team in the spring and take a three-week trip to Germany with his high school German class that summer, and he wanted to run cross-country in college. I was afraid he would never be able to do any of these things. To Chad's credit and through his determination and hard work, he was able to do all three.

The one change that was difficult for me was letting go of my worrying about Chad. We agreed during his partial hospitalization treatment program that we could ask questions on Sunday afternoons, but other days were off limits for questions. That helped satisfy my curiosity about how he was doing, and he only had to answer questions one day a week. This agreement continued after he was released from the hospital and we participated in the follow-up treatment.

Chad is still the terrific kid he always was; he's just wiser and stronger. On the day we left him at the hospital, he said he'd never be able to talk with anyone about his ordeal. This summer, before he left for pre-season college cross-country practice, he called his high school cross-country coach and asked for a chance to speak with the entire boys and girls team about all he'd experienced. How powerful that must have been for those kids to hear Chad—an excellent student, an excellent runner, the captain of the team his senior year—talk about what he dealt with when no one else was really aware of why he missed six or seven weeks of school! He also was able to convince another high school student, one he didn't even know, to get treatment after his mother called me (at the suggestion of Chad's high school counselor).

Chad also learned to trust people. Because his evaluation and hospitalization occurred right at semester exam time last year, Chad was terrified that others would find out; he was afraid that kids at school would tease him and that teachers would think less of him, as he put it. As a teacher myself, I tried to explain that teachers would only think, "Wow. Chad is a terrific kid. Why did this have to happen to him?" (Incidentally, that's exactly what happened.) I insisted on calling all his teachers together to explain what was going on, and I explained that their staying mum about Chad's situation was critical to his recovery. They were wonderful. They simply told inquiring students that Chad had some heart problems (it was true), and that until doctors were comfortable with his recovery, he would not be allowed home. In addition, his best friend, family members, and the one other friend he trusted never once betrayed his confidence. Only when he was strong enough and comfortable enough with it all did he begin to tell others.

I'm delighted to have the "old" Chad back. He laughs, spends time with friends again, teases, gives me a hug for no reason, is enjoying life at college—including his running—and is once again feeling in control.

What did I lose because of the eating disorder? Good question. I know I lost a lot of sleep! I also lost a few months of "normalcy"—driving hours to the hospital and back, ferrying homework assignments to and from Chad's school. Looking back, it seems a blur. But what a small price to pay for Chad's health and well-being.

What did I gain? A new respect for the insidiousness of this disorder. I don't think one can understand how powerful it is unless one has been through it. I even talked with doctors at our local clinic this summer, hoping they would consider doing more specific education on eating disorders with their staff. I believe our doctor missed some important signs, and I don't think he knew what to look for.

My advice? Get help. Talk with someone who knows what to do. Don't assume the person with the disorder will be able to take care of it alone. It'll take time and hard work, but it can be overcome, so don't give up! And trust that there will be some good that comes out of it all.

*I still don't pretend to understand everything about why this happened to my son, but as a father, I know now that by not casting judgment on him—and by loving him all the more for what he was enduring—we were able to get through the tears...*

*—Sean*

# Chad's Dad, Sean

*Sean was integrally involved in his son's treatment program and recovery. The excerpts of Sean's insights, which follow, are addressed directly to the parents of children with eating disorders. He calls to mind some key parenting principles that fathers or mothers can sometimes forget—especially in the face of their child's illness and struggles.*

What I would say first of all is trust your instincts. If you think that there might be a problem, there probably is! We had taken our son to the doctor locally on two or three occasions for what we thought were some minor medical issues (for instance, dark-colored skin on the hands and rapid weight loss). The doctor assured us that everything was fine. Later, when we noticed Chad's unusual eating habits, we finally went on our own and made an appointment for an initial assessment at an eating disorders treatment program. I remember sitting in the waiting area that morning before the visit and talking with my wife about the worst-case scenario—which, in our minds, translated into having some medication for a few weeks. We were shocked to find out that our son needed to be admitted that very day because he was in poor health. As the treatment team explained it, he was at a point where we "could try to awaken him one morning, and he would be gone."

As a parent, I went through all the emotions of guilt ("How could I not see this happening?"), denial ("This can't be happening to us!"), and anger ("Why my child?"). We found out later that these reactions were normal for parents of children with eating disorders, but we were so glad that we could have a treatment team on hand to support us. They helped us deal with all the emotions that accompanied this scary time.

The second thing I would remind parents to do is love your child unconditionally. Our son was in the middle of his senior year of high school. He trained hard the previous summer for that fall's cross-country season. Losing weight and running faster seemed logical to him at the time. He knew something was wrong but would not confide in us that he had a problem. It was hard to not take that lack of trust personally. I still don't pretend to understand everything about why this happened to my son, but as a father, I know now that by not casting judgment on him—and by loving him all the more for what he was enduring—we were able to get through the tears (both his and mine!).

Finally, remember that there is hope. Our son was admitted to an eating disorders treatment program exactly one year ago this week. He is currently in college and is involved in both cross-country and track. As a result of Chad's ordeal, we have learned a tremendous amount about ourselves—not only as a family but as individuals. As a father, I know my son better and am very proud of what he has accomplished for himself. Do I wish that he wouldn't have had to go through this experience? Of course. Am I glad that the treatment program was there when we needed it? Absolutely! I can only hope that you have a similar successful experience if the need arises for your son or daughter.

*Every time you meet a situation,*
*though you think at the time it is an impossibility*
*and you go through the torture of the damned,*
*once your have met it and lived through it,*
*you find that forever after*
*you are freer than you were before.*

*—Eleanor Roosevelt*

*I know it sounds strange, but the struggle that I had in fighting the eating disorder increased my self-confidence and my own self-esteem, to the point that I came out stronger, more aware of myself and what I am capable of doing.*

*—Tara*

# Tara

When I was younger, primarily in my preteen years, I was always overweight. I think the most I weighed was 185 pounds. My mom would always be saying things to me about my weight, and my doctor was meanwhile reminding my mom that I needed to shed pounds. I tried many different times to lose weight, but nothing ever worked. Then one day, I got an incentive. There was a certain pair of jeans—I think they were Girbaud—that I wanted my mom to buy for me. They were very expensive jeans, about eighty-five dollars a pair. I asked her if I could get them and she said, "I'm not spending eighty-five dollars on a pair of jeans if you are going to grow out of them; I will buy you those jeans if you can get down to 140 pounds." So shortly after Christmas, at the age of twelve, I began seriously dieting. I started with a plan of eating one meal a day. I ate one bowl of cereal in the morning—that's all. That went on for a week. Then one day I was headed to my locker at school, and I got extremely lightheaded. I sat down and said, "Okay, one meal may not be enough. I'll do two meals, and that's it." And so from January until about April, I ate two meals a day. I always ate breakfast and I would eat lunch at school. If I didn't eat lunch at school, I would eat dinner. I had talked to my mom about that plan, so if I didn't eat dinner, she assumed I ate lunch, and if I was eating dinner, she assumed I didn't eat lunch.

"As long as you are eating two meals a day, that's okay," she said.

And then I started walking. It was still winter, so I would only walk a mile a day. Then when spring came, I started walking more. I ended up walking four miles a day by the end of March. By April, three or four months after starting my diet, I had gone from 185 pounds to 130 pounds. I was flying high as far as how I felt emotionally. I couldn't believe I could actually lose all that weight. I got the Girbaud jeans. I had soccer and dance practice, and I was walking every day. Even though I was eating only two meals a day, I still had all this energy. I felt really good.

One day, my mom picked me up from school. When I got in the car, she told me that she was really happy with where I had gotten. "You don't need to go any further," she said. "You look good the way you are, and I hope that you feel good too—you seem like you are happy and everything—and you don't need to lose any more weight. You've done a phenomenal job."

I heard everything that she said. But I remember what I felt in response: "I don't *need* to lose more weight, but I can. I'm not done yet. I can get to 125 pounds."

So as the school year ended, I began increasing my walks to twice a day. I went to the mall and picked up a couple of books on losing weight and cutting calories. One book listed the fat and calorie content for every possible food you can imagine. With my mom being gone during the day and my dad sleeping during the day (he worked the night shift), no one was really around to watch what I did. I was thirteen at the time. I ended up heavily restricting my calorie intake and walked four miles two times a day—once early in the morning, before my mom got up, and once in the early afternoon. In the middle of those walks, I would do two-and-a-half hours of aerobics. I would go grocery shopping with my mom and make her buy me low-calorie and low-fat foods.

I started out the summer with a diet of 1,800 calories a day. Then it went to 1,500, then 1,000. By July of 1993, I was eating only 500 calories a day. I remember instances when my mom would say, "You have to eat." If she walked out of the room, I would take a banana, peel it, throw the banana in the garbage, and then throw the peel in the garbage just as she was coming back into the room. So it looked like I had eaten, but I hadn't.

One night, my mom made me sit down and eat an entire meal. I cried throughout the entire thing. When I was done, I was miserable and took an entire sheet of laxatives—for the first and last time—and stormed out of the house to walk my usual four miles. That's when my mom called the doctor to get me some help. A couple of days later, I was admitted to the hospital in my hometown.

I was admitted to the pediatric floor. I did laps around the nurses' desk with my IV pole. I had fights with the dietitian (I still need to go back there and apologize to her). On my third day there, I got a phone call from the doctor. He called to tell me that this particular hospital could not help me anymore, that I was going to be sent to a bigger city for treatment, and that my mom was going to be there soon to pick me up. I knew nothing about this because my mom had not told me. All I could picture was me locked up in a jail cell with this Thanksgiving dinner all around me and being forced to stay in the cell until I ate it all. I was freaking out. I cried the whole way to the treatment center.

I was diagnosed with anorexia nervosa and major depression and was also found to be a compulsive exerciser. I stayed at the treatment center as an inpatient for six or seven weeks. And slowly, I began to get better. What was most helpful for me during my inpatient stay were the one-on-one check-ins with the nurse, during which a nurse would sit down with me for forty-five minutes and go over educational books (about anorexia, for instance). I needed the goals and the strategy planning, so these educational sessions not only increased my knowledge as far as what was happening to my body, but they also made me think about if I really wanted this eating disorder in my life, and what I needed to do to get rid of it.

Before treatment, I had always had an obsession with having an ultra-flat stomach. One day during my treatment, a couple of weeks after being admitted to the center, my mom called. I told her that just that morning, I woke up and looked at my stomach. "It looks a bit fuller," I told her, "but it's okay." My mom said that she thought that this was a good sign—and that she hoped it would last.

For once, I felt like someone was caring. I am a middle child, and I always felt like I had to be perfect for my parents. I am and can still be a perfectionist in different ways, but I've learned that I can't treat perfection like a life-or-death situation. During certain evenings while I was in treatment, I would receive assignments. The assignments often consisted of goal-setting, strategy-building, journaling, or activities to work on body image. The morning after these tasks were given, someone would come to my room and say, "Okay, I want to know where you are with this assignment—what you have done and how you feel about your progress." There was continual follow-through, and in the process of their caring, I learned that I did not have to be so perfect about things all the time.

I also wanted to get better because of the reality of how sick I really was. Shortly before I was admitted to the hospital, I had a doctor's appointment and learned that my pulse was 32 and I had an abnormal electrocardiogram. When I was in inpatient treatment, my primary care doctor from my hometown came to visit me. "Did you know that if you would not have gotten up here—if we would have waited until the appointment that your mom had scheduled two-and-a-half weeks later—you might not be here right now?" he asked. "Do you understand where your heart was then?" I was getting the facts straight, and that combination of honesty, caring, education, and awareness about how sick I was is what got me to want to get better no matter what.

It was hard to get back to a normal weight. But the treatment team was extremely supportive as I struggled with the control that numbers had over me. When school ended in May 1993, I was 125 pounds. By the time I was admitted to my hometown hospital, I was 88 pounds. When I left the treatment center I was at 105. I remember the doctor did not want me to leave until I was at that weight. I remember crying when he told me that. "What is the big fear about 105?" he said. "You are giving power to numbers." Although it was difficult to grasp at that time, those words really helped me realize what I was doing.

When I got out of treatment, I went home. My mom had it set up so that I could continue a six-meal-a-day eating plan. I would get up and have breakfast with my mom before she went to work. My dad, who was still working nights, would be home by the time I had to have a snack, and he would stay up and have lunch with me. My sister was home from school by the time I had my afternoon snack, and then the whole family would have dinner with me. Then my mom would join me for an evening snack. This meal pattern took place on days that I wasn't in school. It got a bit harder to do on the days I was in school, but for the most part, I was able to stick to it. For about a month and half, I ate with someone.

When I went back to school, the hardest part was that everybody was talking about me, and I mean everybody. I had a friend come up to me and say, "You know, you look like someone that I know, but I don't know if she is still going to this school or not."

"Really, who?" I asked her.

"Tara L—," she said. And that's when I told her that I was who she was inquiring about. I will never forget the look on her face.

And there I was, in school, looking like a Chia Pet because I was so cold and the hairs were just sticking up off my arms. The teachers were letting me go grab my jacket, and other people were saying, "I'm cold now, but I can't wear my jacket. Why can she?" I just felt singled out.

When I got home from the first day of school, a friend of mine called, "just to warn" me. This is what so-and-so is saying about you, and this is what so-and-so is saying about what you did; she went on and on. My next-door neighbor, another supposed friend, was saying that I had just done it for attention. I cut all ties with her. (Her parents still live next door to my parents. We will say "hi" to each other now if we see each other, but to this day, I think about how a lifelong friendship just went down the drain.) My mom came home that night, and I cried and cried to her, telling her I did not want to go back. "Bring me back to the hospital right now," I said. "I don't want to be here."

My mom was supportive but firm. "You are going to have to face it at one time or another," she said. "Are you going to do it now, or are you going to wait?"

On the second day of school, our class pictures were taken. At that time, my face and body was so thin; you could see the veins going down my neck. I didn't want to be remembered for the eating disorder. So in November, my parents let me have professional photos done, and I submitted one to the school. They put that photo in the yearbook instead.

Throughout my eating disorder, my parents made it clear to me at all times that I was not alone, and that's what helped me ultimately recover. I never had to be hospitalized again. Before I was discharged from the hospital, my mom and I made an agreement that if she saw me slipping, she would tell me face to face. If she saw me going backward at all, she would tell me—whether I liked it or not. As I mentioned earlier, when I was discharged from the hospital, I was 105 pounds. A week later, when I went to the doctor, I was down to 97 pounds. I was probably running around more than I should have been because I was assisting a coach in soccer, and I liked the game. But my brother made a comment to my mom about it, stating that I wasn't looking so great. True to her word, my mom sat down and talked with me about it.

My mom had taken all the scales out of the house before I had been discharged. I don't think they even have one to this day. Removing the scales from the house was probably one of the best things my mom could have done. I was so focused on numbers and what my weight was at that time, and not having the option to weigh myself multiple times a day removed one of the eating disorder's biggest triggers. I was basically forced to trust others and my meal plan and to focus more on how I felt energy-wise and emotionally—without the power I had given to numbers. While I was living with the active eating disorder, whatever number appeared on the scale made or broke my day—or even hour—and it was not unusual for me to weigh myself a dozen times a day. Currently I don't own a scale, nor do I want one. I will admit that if I am going to the doctor, that is the one thing I find myself getting anxious about it at times: "What is the scale going to read?" That's when I remind myself, "Does it really matter?"

Today, I am fully recovered from my eating disorder and have been for about eight years. I just finished my bachelor of science degree in nursing and passed my registered nursing boards in July. I also have a minor in psychology. I am planning on continuing to graduate school to get my master of science degree in advanced-practice nursing and specialize in psychiatric nursing. I am currently contemplating working toward a career as a psychiatric nurse practitioner or psychiatric nurse specialist.

I like the way that I look now. I am comfortable with my body. But it was not like that right away after treatment. For some time, I wore wide-leg dress pants and looser tops because I felt like I wanted to dress comfortably. About five years ago, however, my mom noticed that I was wearing more "fitting" clothes.

"How do you feel?" she asked.

"I like the way that they fit," I told her. "I like how they look on me."

"That's probably one of the best things I have heard come out of your mouth," she said.

I have a funny story to share about the support I received. My parents remained vigilant about my health after I was discharged from the hospital (they do to this day, of course, although I am no longer living at home). About a year after coming home from treatment, I asked my dad if I could get a membership to a gym. Both of my parents were skeptical. My dad went in and talked to the people at the gym and signed a contract with them. This contract stipulated that if I was there for more than two hours, he'd come and get me and I may be kicked out. (I was not aware of this contract.) One day, I decided to go to an aerobics class and then sit in the hot tub. All of a sudden, my eyes turned toward the entrance to the pool and there was my dad!

"Dad! Hi!" I said.

"There you are," he said. "I told you that if you're here for over two hours, I am going to pick you up."

"I'm just using the hot tub."

"Well, I'm happy you're here. Now come on out before you turn into a prune."

It was touching to know that he was keeping an eye on me—even though he did not necessarily need to at that point. The thought of being too active—to help the eating disorder—just wasn't there anymore.

In having an eating disorder, I gained more respect for myself. I know it sounds strange, but the struggle that I had in fighting the eating disorder increased my self-confidence and my own self-esteem, to the point that I came out stronger, more aware of myself and what I am capable of doing. This strength is what keeps the eating disorder from gaining any momentum during the events in which I might be considered weak or vulnerable—for instance, during "swimsuit season."

To the people supporting someone with an eating disorder, I would say, be strong. Don't give up on your loved one. Realize, even in the midst of your frustration, that you are angry or upset not with your loved one but with what the eating disorder is making him or her do. Stay present, and don't lose your connection as a family member or friend.

If you have an eating disorder, know that there is a better life out there. Do not give up no matter how frustrated you get with yourself, no matter how many times you may feel you are turning around and going backward. And never cut ties with the people who are truly supporting you. You may think that they are out to do more harm than good, but they are actually helping you more than you can acknowledge at this moment. When you are stronger and the eating disorder has left you, you will be able to realize it.

If you can't run, then walk. If you can't walk, then crawl. But by all means necessary, don't stop moving forward.

Remember that there is no "perfect;" the perfection that the eating disorder is striving for does not and never will exist.

*Tara is now twenty-three years old. She is currently working as a registered nurse at a hospital.*

## *Trust Yourself*

*Trust in yourself*
*to know what is right*
*Know*
*that this is your truth*
*Listen with open mind and heart*
*to your deepest needs*
*and desires*
*Be not ashamed*
*to seek out your life*

*With the wind gently*
*grazing your face*
*teasing your hair*
*tickling your neck*
*And the moon*
*brightly shining*
*piercing clouds*
*penetrating darkness*
*Your deepest fears emerged*

*Be grateful for life*
*Look kindly upon yourself*
*made with the same hands*
*grown from the same seeds*
*as the earth*
*Listen to the wind*
*Trust in the guiding light of the moon*

*Smile*
*Love yourself*

*—Christine*
*(former patient of an eating*
*disorders treatment program)*

*When recovery came into view, I began to focus just on the present and what I was gaining back... I had the opportunity to reunite with what I once had—and connect with a more positive future.*

*—Teresa*

# Teresa

I guess I would say that my eating disorder began when I was fifteen. I was transitioning to high school, and I was trying to get in better shape for the volleyball season, and so I thought that if I ate fewer snack foods, I would be faster and quicker. I figured it wouldn't hurt just to cut out a few things here and there. Eventually, I was cutting back on the foods I needed to eat, in hopes of toning my body. I went from feeling really good to feeling not so healthy.

I had some of the characteristic qualities of someone with an eating disorder. I was the only girl in my family, and I always seemed to want to do everything right; I was a perfectionist. I wanted to do well in volleyball because my dad was really into us being athletic, and he was always cheering us on, always at our games, and I did not want to disappoint him. I did not want to get in trouble, so I always had good grades and never did any of the rebellious things that teens do—like drinking, smoking, staying out past curfew. Doing something wrong was just not what I wanted to do. The eating disorder made me feel like I could have control over something. At the time, I thought it was something that I could do for myself that would make me better. What ended up happening is that my "healthier" eating habits snowballed out of control. I kept losing more and more weight, and while I felt I was in control, I really wasn't.

In February of 1993, when I was seventeen, my family and I went to Cancún. They realized—looking at me in a swimsuit—how much weight I had lost. And I felt weak. I remember it was difficult to play volleyball on the beach. I put up a front that I could actually play, but it was tough to jump and hit the ball because my arms were so much thinner. I know on the trip I didn't eat a lot, and my parents took notice of that.

When we got back from our trip, my parents intervened. At first, the doctor in my hometown sent me to a mental health unit, because I was more depressed than anything. Then I began to see a pediatrician in a different city, and I ended up having to have a feeding tube. It was embarrassing to be there—sitting in a bed on the pediatric floor next to a three-year-old, with a tube up my nose. The freakiness of it scared me enough to want to eat—to do whatever I could to get out of there. I just told myself to do what it took to get out, and then I could do whatever I wanted to again. It was the typical mentality of a person who is suffering from an eating disorder.

Shortly after that hospital stay, I began to be treated for my eating disorder at a clinic that specializes in it. At that point, I was frustrated with my home life because my parents seemed to always be on my case about things, and I really felt at the time that they weren't connecting with me on anything. And so in my senior year of high school, I asked my grandfather if I could come live with him and my grandmother. They agreed, and I changed schools. I figured that it would be a clean, fresh start. It was liberating to be my own person, and I got along wonderfully with the people at my new school, but I couldn't enjoy the experience fully because I was always tired and distracted and I just felt numb—all because of the eating disorder. I couldn't really fully experience emotions. I was in the world, yet I wasn't.

I seemed just to be going through the motions. Although moving appeared to be a positive step, I was still restricting my intake of food. And meanwhile, my parents were looking in from the outside, seeing my grandparents raise me, and it bothered my mom so much. She was devastated by it. In my devious, eating-disordered mind, I was saying, "See? Now, if you had treated me right, I would still be living at home." It was as though I was a completely different person. I went through my senior year feeling on the edge.

The deception carried into my treatment program, too—at least for a while. I was getting weighed by my family doctor, who didn't know anything about eating disorders. So I would hide weights on myself. It was unbelievable. That's how desperate and out of touch I was. Eventually, they found out that I was hiding bags of coins in my sweatshirt to make the scale read heavier, and they made me take off all of my clothes when being weighed. Everyone realized then how critical my situation was. I literally could have keeled over and died, yet all I cared about was making sure I could fool people.

In college, I began a cycle of receiving treatment, then dropping out (usually because I didn't do what I was supposed to), then being readmitted, then dropping out again. In a way, treatment was a safety net during that time. "If I get sick enough, they'll put me in a hospital, and then I won't have to worry about myself anymore," I thought. I didn't think about how getting better would help me gain control of my life. In January of 1996, I was admitted to a regional mental hospital based on a judge's ruling, which in and of itself was a scary thing. I knew at that point that I wasn't getting out until I had gained a certain amount of weight and maintained it. And for a while, that was a horrible situation. I thought I would be there forever. I thought that there was nowhere else I could turn, no one would take me back. Then, I set a goal. I planned on going to college that fall, and I was accepted at a college and had received a scholarship, so I set my mind to it. I got up to my goal weight and I maintained it so that I could be discharged.

It was not until that point—where I had gained weight and was being physically nourished—that I realized what I was missing out on. I remember taking a walk and thinking, "This is crazy. All of my former high school classmates are graduating from college; I haven't even started. I have no social life, no friends. This eating disorder was supposed to help me gain a better life, and look at all I have lost." I told myself then and there that I was not going to pass up this huge opportunity to go to school.

I went to school the following fall. But strangely enough, that experience at the state hospital did not even give rise to my "aha" moment. I ended up having to drop out after the first semester because of all the stress, and I just went in the tank. I ended up getting medically stabilized again, and at that point, my parents were at the end of their rope. "We cannot do this anymore," they said. "Emotionally it's been too much for us to take." And at that moment—when I realized that my parents were beside themselves, that no treatment program was going to take me back, that my safety nets were gone, and there was no way I was going back to the hospital—I knew something had to change. I wouldn't say it was overnight, but I remember I was living at home and working part-time, and I just gradually started to eat more. I would write in my journal everything I ate every day, and I was recording more and more foods. And I was proud of that. I would try something new that tasted good, and so I would eat it again. I was starting to reclaim foods on my own. I began to listen to my hunger cues again. And I got to the point where I was pretty comfortable with myself. I started to take little pieces of responsibility for my life. The following year, 1998, I went back to school and began to branch out on my own once again.

I hate to admit it sometimes, but one of the keys to my recovery was the "tough love" moments in my life. My parents learned enough about eating disorders to know how to deal with it, and what ended up working for me was for them not to feed into my negative behaviors and the neediness that followed. My parents read books, talked to people, attended group meetings, and did everything they could to help me. That kind of support from parents and friends and family is key. If someone you love is not educated about the condition—and not involved—it is very, very tough to recover.

During the times when I had an eating disorder, I was withdrawn. I wanted to be alone, didn't want to talk to anybody. As I started to get better, I became more social, and I was willing to put myself out there because I had my confidence and self-esteem back. And even though I wasn't where I needed to be, I did progress. The hardest part was getting over that hump of comparison—looking to the past and then the present and wondering why I couldn't have realized what I was losing sooner, or seeing how everyone else was living their life when it seemed like I was just beginning.

When recovery came into view, I began to focus just on the present and what I was gaining back. I knew then that I could move on with my life and reconnect with people whom I hadn't talked to for a long time. I could face the people who felt guilty and tell them that they were not to blame. I had the opportunity to reunite with what I once had—and connect with a more positive future.

In a way, I am still the same person I was when I had the eating disorder. I am still a little perfectionistic, for example. But when people see me now, they remark to my parents about how much joy I seem to have in my life. And I do have a smile in my eyes. I am talkative and outgoing. I am not isolated and angry any longer. I am close again with my parents and my brother. Our relationship has gotten so much better than I ever expected, and I know that we will always love each other and will do anything for each other. And sure, I may seem to be on the slow track as I watch many of my friends getting married and having children, while I just graduated from college two years ago. But it doesn't matter to me because I have still accomplished something great: I am still here, I am alive, I'm doing well, and I'm still young. It soothes me inside to know that.

I still have stressful experiences—involving relationships and dating, for instance—but I know now that I would never go back to the eating disorder again. Today, I know that whatever path I take in life, it will work out. It may not be easy, but I have my optimism. Having been through this journey—and having survived—I can pretty much set my mind to doing whatever it is I want to do.

My wish for anyone who has an eating disorder is that you would know that recovery is truly possible. When you are sick with an eating disorder, it is so hard to understand that you can recover. Of course you have to be recovered to know that you can recover, but I still wish that I could give you that gift of knowing your own determination and strength. Believe in yourself, seriously. Seek support from people, sure, but learn how to find out who you are—because ultimately, the healing is all up to you.

*Teresa graduated from college with a degree in psychology. She is currently single and has embarked on a new adventure by moving to Maryland, near Baltimore.*

*I think overall that Teresa's anorexia was the best thing that happened to our family—even though it was a very rough time. It seems ironic. We are all more open about our feelings and know that life is precious.*

*—Bridget*

# Teresa's Mom, Bridget

*For some family members of individuals with an eating disorder, talking about the ordeal—no matter how much time has passed, no matter how wholly their child or sister or brother has healed—is inordinately difficult. During the production of this book, we interviewed many parents and siblings of those with eating disorders. Two such people were Bridget and Jeffrey, Teresa's parents. The more they talked about their daughter's previous struggles, the more they found that the discussion itself could unleash sadness, guilt, anger—all of the emotions that come with enduring, and overcoming, a family loss or crisis. Days after the interview, Teresa's mom sent us this letter, which eloquently captures the quandaries that many parents face as they support their child's own journey toward hope, healing, and ultimately, recovery.*

When Teresa was going through her eating disorder, it was a very hard time for me, and talking about those times brought back the memories of what our family went through...

Early on in Teresa's illness, what was frustrating for me as a mom was that I wanted to help my daughter but didn't know how. As a parent, you always want your children to be healthy and happy. Teresa's illness left me helplessly searching for the right thing to say or do. As a parent, you want to fix or help your children with their problems. What was disappointing to me was watching Teresa go from a happy, fun-loving, caring person to someone slowly trying to kill herself—and knowing that she had a lot of determination but was letting the anorexia take over her life. I did a lot of praying and had many sleepless nights. As I lay awake, I would ask myself where I went wrong as a mom.

Teresa's relapses were disappointing, too. She was very smart and manipulative—not only in treatment, but also when she came home. I tried not to watch her or ask her if she had eaten. But it was not easy, and consequently, we got into many arguments over the anorexia. My relationship with Jeffrey was also suffering. I knew how much he was hurting inside. He was very patient and always seemed to be there when times got rough. But financially, we were strapped, and this added to our stress.

I think the hardest part, besides wanting to help Teresa get better, was trying to keep a normal family life. I would go to work and try to get through the day without crying, for fear someone would ask me how she was doing. I knew that everyone was only trying to be considerate, but that awareness did not help. When I would go somewhere and people were laughing and enjoying themselves, I would say to myself, "Why is our family going through this ordeal while other families are having a normal life?" I was even on antidepressants for a few months to help me cope. After about three years, I finally realized I did nothing wrong as a mom and that it was out of my control whether Teresa got better. After that time, normal activity seemed easier for me.

It was a challenge for me to be positive during Teresa's treatment because she continued to have relapses. The treatment teams were all doing their job, but Teresa was not helping herself. Every time she went to treatment, I prayed that this time would be the last time. She would start to recover, but then she would relapse. The anorexia seemed to get stronger and stronger.

After Teresa's ten months in the state mental hospital and her return home, it was really a "tough love" situation. It was difficult, but we basically told her if she continued letting the anorexia take over her life, she would no longer be allowed to live in our home. I believe she realized that we were serious, and she needed to get on with her life. It took a few months, but things eventually began to improve. As Teresa got better, my relationship with her got better. Knowing that I could once again feel like a mom was a gradual process. Slowly, Teresa began to be more social and have a better outlook on life. She was looking ahead to college, which was positive. She connected with her psychiatrist and got a job. It seemed strange, but our family life became somewhat normal after such a long time.

During Teresa's illness, our extended family was very helpful and supportive. I think they and also our friends wanted to help, but they didn't know how. They did help in caring for our son if we needed to be with Teresa. And Teresa did live with her grandparents her senior year of high school. As I look back, I feel that it was not good for me because I missed out on many of Teresa's school events. I remember just thinking, "I will do whatever it takes to help her get better." The positive side was that Teresa found a talent for singing and acting during this time.

It was difficult on our son during Teresa's illness. He was angry and confused, not knowing if his sister would survive. They rarely spoke to each other. He had trouble in school with grades and discipline. I think he was rebelling. He and Teresa now have a good relationship; they even lived together for a year after they both finished college!

I think overall that Teresa's anorexia was the best thing that happened to our family—even though it was a very rough time. It seems ironic. We are all more open about our feelings and know that life is precious.

For other families going through an eating disorder, I would say the following: Be patient. Pray a lot and be there for your loved one. Try to find a support group. Read and gather as much information about eating disorders as you can.

As for Teresa, she has since graduated from college (which was a very special day), has more self-confidence, has her sense of humor back, is forming new relationships, supports herself financially, and loves to try new restaurants! In my eyes, Teresa is the bravest person in the world for beating anorexia. I now have my happy, fun-loving, and caring daughter back. I do believe that miracles can happen.

*As parents, I believe we have learned some things...*
*We understand the value of patience. We realize that*
*it's okay to ask for help. We know that above all,*
*we have to be there for our children.*
*We have to stick by them, even when it hurts.*

*—Jeffrey*

# Teresa's Dad, Jeffrey

Although Teresa's eating disorder began in 1992, it was quite some time before we actually knew about it. Teresa's best friend had told Teresa's volleyball coach, and then the volleyball coach went to the counselor, who told the school nurse, who told us. At first, the nurse thought that she was depressed, so she suggested that Teresa see a psychiatrist. The psychiatrist quickly discovered it was an eating disorder. By the time Teresa was officially diagnosed, it was March of 1993.

I was shocked to hear this news. I had never heard of anorexia in my life. Then suddenly, I learned my daughter had it. Her friends called and said that rather than eating at the school cafeteria, she was spending her lunch hour in the hallways. When her friends asked her to go out, she would refuse. She stayed home more. She wore baggy clothes.

Up to that time, everything seemed fine. Teresa and her brother were close, and as parents, we tried to be involved in their activities. Teresa played volleyball, and she was doing well at it. I couldn't understand why or how this was happening.

I was thankful that her best friend was aware of the illness and brought it to the attention of Teresa's volleyball coach. Had she not come forward, Teresa's disease could have gone on for a long time without our ever knowing it.

The news of Teresa's eating disorder threw us into a tizzy for a time. We thought, "We'll take her to the hospital, and everything will be taken care of. She'll be back at volleyball or whatever she wants to do with her life." We were mistaken. As parents, we would think about how it started and why, and who or what was at fault. All at once, there was this blame to pass around. Of course, it was really no one's fault that Teresa had an eating disorder, but it took a long time to realize that.

The eating disorder added chaos to our lives. Our son is five years younger than Teresa, and he was just getting active in a lot of school activities such as basketball, baseball, school dances, things of that nature. It was challenging during those first couple months of Teresa's treatment to have enough time to do things with him. I still can't help feeling that he was a little bit cheated, even though I know we did the best we could do. We had a lot of people supporting us. My brother and his wife watched our son whenever we needed them. Bridget's mother and father also helped out, as did my mother and father. They all spent time with our son so we could devote more time to Teresa's illness. After Teresa's first treatment, I thought, "Huh, okay. This is done." I did not know at the time that the road to recovery can be long.

I kept pretty good records of Teresa's illness—her times in and out of treatment. Over the course of five years, she was in eight or nine different outpatient or inpatient programs. The final treatment that Teresa received was in a regional mental health facility in our area. Some programs she was in two or three times.

During Teresa's treatment, we met frequently with the treatment professionals to talk about Teresa's progress. For the most part, Teresa was not honest with the treatment team. She was manipulative, and she had the system figured out. She knew what to do to make it seem like she was recovering when she really wasn't. Where she learned it from, I have no idea. She was smart enough to outwit her treatment team, yet she was not smart enough to know that what she was doing to herself just had to stop. Had she been healthy, she probably could have figured it all out. But the illness took over, and she was too sick to understand what was happening. As a result, she was not the greatest patient. Every time we put her into a new program, we would think, "Okay, this time it will help." But that time wouldn't work, so we would go to the next program. She wasn't gaining anything; she never stopped to determine what it was that she was getting out of each program. And every time she got out, she would automatically start losing more weight.

The whole cycle of Teresa's going in and out of treatment, of losing weight again and again, made me feel helpless and worthless. I thought, "I should be able to fix this problem—or at least find someone who can." We thought we had been sending her to the best doctors, including those who specialized in eating disorders, and even they could not do anything.

As parents, it was tough to determine how best to cope. There were really no support groups in our area at the time, and there weren't too many families in our town who had dealt with eating disorders. At one point, we did attend a Saturday support group through one of the hospitals where Teresa was receiving treatment, and that was very helpful. We also bought whatever books we could find on the subject and tried to find other families who had gone through eating disorders.

Despite the support that we were receiving, I realized in time how isolating it can be to have a child with an eating disorder. After a while, for instance, my friends started shying away from me. They quit asking me to do things with them—mostly because they probably didn't know what to ask or what to say anymore. I suppose that they got sick of asking how Teresa was doing, and I got sick of answering, to be honest. I think it was hard for them to talk to me without hurting my feelings, and rather than risking looking foolish, they just kind of excluded me from activities. We also didn't have a lot of time to do things with our friends because when we weren't with Teresa, we were trying to make up some time with our son.

We carried many other burdens as a result of the eating disorder. Teresa's brother was feeling anger toward his sister and would not attend any family events. (It remained touchy until about five or six years ago, when Teresa started to get better.) The insurance companies, meanwhile, would not cover more than thirty days of any one treatment, so we became a bit strapped financially. I was in a business partnership and was taking a lot of time off work to deal with Teresa's illness, and I felt guilty about that. It was a tough five years, and I would not wish it on anybody—especially kids.

I am not sure why it took Teresa five years to recover from the eating disorder. I am not sure if she wanted to get better at first because she didn't think it was a real problem. She thought she could survive without eating, that she could eat when she wanted to—but she couldn't. I wondered sometimes how she was surviving.

Probably what was most frustrating and disappointing about Teresa's illness is what she was missing out on. She went through her eating disorder when she was in the prime of her teenage years, when she could have been out running around and having fun with her friends and doing all her high school activities. Instead, she missed out on those times, and that really got to me. After she got out, she tried to make up for lost time, but it was too late, in my opinion. Her high school years were over.

Another challenging part was when Bridget and I would be in town and we would see Teresa's friends doing fun things together, attending sporting events, going to school plays, going out to the local pizza place to hang out with friends. I would see Teresa's friends' parents and they would say, "Oh, Jane is in college at 'such and such,'" or "Susie just graduated and took a job with 'so and so.'" And I would think, "Well yeah, my daughter is sitting in the hospital somewhere." It was so hard. The whole experience really made me a negative person for a while.

One of the most miserable years for us was when Teresa went to live with her grandparents. We had received some bad advice from a doctor, who said that it was important for Teresa to let her make her own decisions, and because Teresa wanted to move to change schools, we thought it would work out. During that year, Teresa had these big events for school, such as the prom, and Bridget missed out on experiencing all of those big occasions with her daughter. It was tough on Bridget and me as parents.

It may sound sad, but at some point, I pretty much had given up on the idea that Teresa would ever get better. It was taking so long, and her attitude was so negative for such a long time that I did not think she would ever, ever get out of it. She was always blaming someone else; it was always someone else's fault.

But one day, Teresa did start to get better. And it came on so fast, seemingly overnight. It happened after she was released from the mental hospital, where she had been in treatment for ten months. When she came home, we told her pretty much flat-out that if she didn't get better, she couldn't live with us. I was scared, and I was figuring that she would be lapsing back into the same unhealthy behavior again. We essentially resorted to a "tough love" approach. I can tell you, the toughest thing that you could ever tell your child is that he or she is not welcome at home. But Bridget and I were desperate.

Teresa took the warnings seriously. She connected with a psychiatrist whom she really liked, and she got a job. She saw her friends graduating from college, and she was just starting to recover. I think she just said, "Enough is enough." She did a lot of work in a hurry. She started school at a junior college in our hometown, and after her first year there, realizing how happy she was, she enrolled in a private college. Once she got going, she didn't give the eating disorder any space. She knew what she had to do. She was strong in that way, and as she gained some ground, she got even stronger. She never went back to the eating disorder.

I wondered, once Teresa started to recover, why it was that she waited so long—why she couldn't have done it five years before. But I was glad that she did it when she did.

I wish I could provide some advice for parents who are going through this type of experience. But I don't know what to tell anyone, really. The only thing I can say is to be prepared for a long haul. Recovery does not happen overnight, and in fact, it may take years. But it can happen.

Bridget and I try not to talk about the eating disorder too much with Teresa. But I do think about it. I don't know if other parents are like this, but I always think that something could still happen—and that the eating disorder could return. I don't dwell on it daily, but there are times when I am alone, or I learn that she is having a bad day, and I wonder if she is doing okay. But at this point everything is fine, so I must trust, too.

Having recovered from an eating disorder, Teresa now knows that she can overcome crises—and that if she sets her mind to it, she can do anything. As parents, I believe we have learned some things, too. We understand the value of patience. We realize that it's okay to ask for help. We know that above all, we have to be there for our children. We have to stick by them, even when it hurts.

Every once in a while, we get a call from the parent of a child who has an eating disorder. Even though we don't have any easy answers, we try to help as much as we can—just as all of our friends and family members helped us when Teresa was going through it. We are giving back now. It may be in just a small way, but it's still a wonderful thing to be doing. It shows me that our family is healing.

*When Teresa began to get better, my own life also changed. All I could think of was, 'I have my sister back!' I look back on those five years when Teresa was sick and feel like I was in a cave.*

*—Peter*

# Teresa's Brother, Peter

When I found out about Teresa's eating disorder, I was shocked, upset, stunned, and disappointed. I truly felt like my family was closed off from the outside world. Her disease seemed to come out of the blue. We were just a regular family living in the comforts of a small town. We had great friendships; we were a loving family.

When I first became aware of the eating disorder, I became very quiet and shy about talking of my sister. There was not a lot of public awareness of eating disorders at that time. I felt that I had failed somehow, somewhere—and had no ability or control to get things back to "normal." I could see myself lying to friends about the problems that our family was having. I was making excuses, and my behavior was not healthy for my mind or body. I began to care less about my own activities, and I did not try as much in classes.

At first, I tried to keep things as quiet as possible so that I did not have to talk about Teresa's illness. Most people did not understand that Teresa's eating disorder was serious. Only close family members and good family friends showed real concern. To others, it seemed like a disease that could quickly be overcome—and something that did not require worry.

As part of Teresa's first round of treatment, my entire family tried family therapy. I went once and told my parents, "Never again," because of how angry I became at my sister. I could not understand for the life of me why she would do this to herself and her family. I wanted a quick answer, and she kept lying and making up what I thought were excuses. I have never been so frustrated and upset.

After Teresa's many hospital stays throughout four or five years, it became clear that she was not getting better. Eventually, no one would take her back, and it became a personal battle for her and my family. Teresa could gain weight back while in treatment, but her mind was in no way ready to get healthy. I saw firsthand how she played the game with the doctors, psychologists, and family—winning every time. The quicker she would gain the weight and get to her target, the quicker she could be released and resume her habits without scrutiny. It was irritating to know that she was released just because she gained ten pounds. Nothing drove me more crazy. I felt completely helpless, and it made me stray from her very quickly.

I visited Teresa occasionally while she was receiving inpatient care, but I had very little, if any, desire to be involved. I wanted more than anyone for Teresa to get better, but I had a strong feeling that my pushing my feelings and anger on her would not help in the least. So I stepped away. Mentally, I almost completely left Teresa. I feel that for many years, I did not have a sister at all.

Another frustration was my not being able to understand how Teresa could work with the treatment afforded her and conquer the minute-to-minute, day-to-day struggles going on in her mind. I got mad when she was unable to answer any question truthfully. I would always become disappointed and embarrassed for her when she was not honest with herself or her family.

With the complexity and range of emotions and issues involved in having a loved one with an eating disorder, it is very difficult to feel supported. I did have family members who wanted to listen and help. But in the end, my biggest support personally came from myself and just having time alone to think. I was able to handle things by growing up fast and using hobbies to escape what I considered a fake world.

Teresa's progress toward healing was extremely slow, painful, and so much more work than anyone thought. Once she felt the desperation of having nowhere else to turn, no one else to go to but herself, she was able to begin to recover. Her physical and mental efforts were extremely rewarding and visible for the first time. I could finally see a change in attitude that was not only sincere but strong enough to beat the internal demons that she seemed to be facing.

About four years into Teresa's illness, I educated myself more about the disease and became comfortable with the knowledge that I had to repair my relationship with my sister. There was also a harder push from my parents to reestablish our relationship. They knew, as I did, that ignoring Teresa and finding fault was not going to be helpful or successful in helping Teresa heal. The following year posed the toughest mental challenge I ever faced. I made a personal vow to become as proactive and hands-on with her as possible. No way, I told myself, would she suffer the rest of her life. No way would she lose this battle.

When recovery came into the picture for Teresa, I witnessed many changes. She had a better attitude toward herself and others. The hair on her head stopped falling out, and the hair on her arms stopped standing up. She ate with her family. She was honest. She did everything opposite from the games she played when she was sick. We were able to communicate again, albeit on a low level.

Her life as a whole changed, too. Teresa was glad to be alive and free again. She had a purpose and drive to prove to herself that she had done something great. She was taking care of herself.

When Teresa began to get better, my own life also changed. All I could think of was, "I have my sister back!" I look back on those five years when Teresa was sick and feel like I was in a cave. It was as though I fell asleep and the world passed me by. (I have never blamed my sister for these feelings, nor would I.) When she began to heal, I became more clear-minded. I began listening more and making an effort to learn about her and the disease. My friendships became more wholesome and meaningful. Time spent with my family meant so much more than it ever did. My ability to talk more openly about problems with my sister and parents made me feel more relaxed and comfortable. Every conversation I had with my sister became sincere, truthful, and meaningful. We learned not to make judgments toward each other.

I know that I have become stronger having gone through the range of emotions I experienced when Teresa was battling her disorder. It may seem like I lost five years, but time is all I have lost. I gained confidence, sincerity, love, independence, and passion. I believe 100 percent that Teresa did not do this for her own reasons. She was simply (but only temporarily) outmatched by something even she has not figured out.

Now that Teresa is living on the East Coast, we don't talk as often, but when we do, the conversations are still upbeat and honest. She is still searching for that perfect job, but she is doing well in the meantime, and she is still independent, strong, and confident. My sister and I love each other more than ever, and we have no embarrassment letting each other know that. I would do anything for her.

For those who have a family member or friend with an eating disorder, I would advise you not to think about what is driving your loved one to follow a path of apparent destruction. Instead, concentrate on finding yourself and your own identity very quickly. Don't let the disease make you someone you are not. Muster all the support—not nagging and blaming—that you can for your family member or friend. Understand your role as best as possible and work on being there for your loved one when it is your time. Treat your loved one like the human being he or she once was, before the whole journey began.

*In a dark time, the eye begins to see.*

*—Theodore Roethke*

*I found my voice by losing the job I loved and felt so competent in. The situation told me that I had to get the eating disorder out of my life because the only person whom I was fooling was myself.*

*—Nora*

# Nora

My eating disorder began when I was fourteen or fifteen, although I was aware of poor body image issues before that. When I was in my early teens, a friend and I figured out that we could binge and purge instead of starving ourselves. The eating disorder took root almost immediately. It was all-consuming. I felt very ashamed.

During the time when I was struggling with the eating disorder, my family seemed to add to the problem. They wanted to help me, but they didn't know how. If they saw vomit in the toilet, they would make a point to tell me how disgusting it was. They tried to be shaming—or "guilt" me into recovery. It wasn't helpful to shame me because I was so disgusted with myself already that it just made me hold on to my eating disorder more tightly.

My eating disorder held me captive for nearly fifteen years. But there came a moment about two years ago when I realized that I needed—and wanted—to get better. I was working for a company as a certified public accountant and believed that I was doing a fabulous job. I was managing six people, and I was so proud of that area of my life. Even though I was purging four times a day, I felt that I was in control and that I was doing well. One day, I was called into the vice president's office, and she told me that she was going to move me over to another area and that I would be a financial analyst. I was devastated. I loved my job and didn't want to have a different position. I asked if I was being demoted, and she said that it was more of a lateral move but that I would no longer have people directly reporting to me. She said that it would be good for my career because I would be more well-rounded. Essentially, I did not have a choice.

I was confused and hurt and didn't understand what was happening. I went for a walk with one of my managers, and he told me that people had been talking and that they felt that I was not very focused and "here." The manager told me that this new position would have less stress and would allow me time to deal with whatever was going on in my life.

I was floored. Here I had thought that I was doing a great job and no one knew about my eating disorder. I was finding out how wrong I was.

At that point, I knew that I could not live with the eating disorder anymore. I transferred to my new job and got involved in a support group for women with eating disorders. With the help of this group and my sister, I stopped bingeing almost immediately and stopped purging gradually. The support group helped me keep myself in check by asking each week whether I binged—and if so, how often and why. When I hadn't binged that week, they were almost as excited as I was. It was thrilling to go there each week with good news, to give the rest of them hope and to get a pat on the back from those who really understood how hard it was. The support group's main function in my recovery was taking away a bit of the shame. I didn't feel like such a freak anymore, because these girls looked like anyone you might see on the street, and they were practicing the same behaviors I was practicing.

As a result of my job transition, I was now in a new work environment that was not conducive to an eating disorder. In my cubicle, everyone knew what I was doing at all times, and the bathrooms near my new work space had automatic toilets that made it very difficult to vomit. I couldn't binge "easily" any longer. That job change (and the accompanying experience) is one of the best things that has ever happened to me.

This is not to say that the whole transition to recovery wasn't challenging. There were many hard times, one of which was telling my husband about my problems and my illness. I had not been honest with him. First, I had to tell him the news about my job, which he did not understand because he thought, like me, that I was doing so well. Second, I had to tell him about my eating disorder. My support group was encouraging me to be honest with him about it, but this was not a simple thing to do. I was afraid. I knew that if he asked me, I could tell him, but I didn't know how to bring it up. I devised a plan with one of the treatment professionals, who called my house one morning after a group session. He talked to my husband and told him that I had left my gloves at the support group meeting the previous evening. After my husband got the phone call, he called me at work. I waited until I got home to tell him everything. At first, he was very supportive and hugged me, but the realization that I had essentially lied to him sunk in, and he became angry. For a while, I didn't know if our relationship would make it, but we have managed to work through it.

I practiced some very strange tactics after eating in order to prevent myself from purging, such as late-night jumping-jack sessions in my closet and lots of sit-ups. I convinced my husband to take walks with me after dinner in order to avoid the panic I often felt with the food just sitting in me. I also worked out every day without fail. It probably wasn't the healthiest way to stop purging, because exercise in itself can be considered a purge sometimes, but it worked for me. Gradually I stopped the immediate need to exercise right after dinner, but I have still made exercise an extremely important part of my recovery.

Things have changed so much since I have overcome the eating disorder. When the eating disorder was present, I was so isolated and really had no life. I had no friends and no life outside of work. Now, I am busy and active and have friends and enjoy doing things with them. I found out that I am likeable. I want to get up each day and extend myself to other people.

I found my voice by losing the job I loved and felt so competent in. The situation told me that I had to get the eating disorder out of my life because the only person whom I was fooling was myself. The eating disorder was providing such a false sense of companionship and support. It offered me nothing, yet it tricked me into thinking it was all I needed.

Today, my life is wonderful. My husband and I are trying to have children, and I have fantastic friends and great relationships with my family. My eating disorder is not in my life at all. I know that if I purge, I will be right back in that cycle. I lost my high school years and my friendships to the eating disorder, but I also gained a compassion and an ability to speak up for myself. I know that I want the life that I have and that if I purge, I will fall back into that lonely, destructive world.

To the people who are going through an eating disorder right now, I would tell you that there is a wonderful world out there, full of color and rich experiences—and that you are missing out on that world because of the eating disorder. To the support person of someone with an eating disorder, I would advise not to badger or shame. It doesn't work, and it turns your loved one toward the eating disorder instead of away from it.

*Nora is now thirty-three years old. She is still a financial analyst and loves it. She and her husband are hoping to start a family soon.*

*Nora is out in the world now, quite the contrast from when the eating disorder was in her life, wrapping a cocoon around her. She is happy.*

*—Laura*

# Nora's Sister, Laura

I don't think I ever understood how bad Nora's eating disorder was until years later, when she was better. It started in her early teenage years with restricting, and she became really thin, so it was obvious that something was going on. She was very sick by the time she was a freshman in college.

My mom always had a weight problem and was very into what was okay to eat and what wasn't. Heaviness ran on my mom's side of the family. As a result, I think that all the women in our family placed way too much emphasis on dieting and losing weight and being thin, because my mom would always be saying things such as, "You don't want to look like us," or "You want to watch what you eat because you don't want what happened to us to happen to you." For some reason, though, this need to be thin hit Nora a lot harder. I was certainly no positive role model for her, either, in terms of my own dieting and focusing on my body at that age. So I felt partially responsible for Nora's illness. I feel bad, even now, that I missed so many signs of the eating disorder for so many years. I wish that I would have been in tune with the symptoms that my sister had—and that I would have said something and done something to help her get better sooner.

We didn't handle Nora's illness well in the beginning. She would get up and leave the table to throw up, and my mom and I handled it so poorly. We tried to guilt her out of it and yell her out of it; "What are you trying to do to everybody?" we would say. It was a stupid way to react, but we didn't know better at that time. We didn't know anything about eating disorders.

Our family life was tumultuous. My dad has bipolar disorder and my parents stayed together despite his illness. So my mom became a tough, wonderful, supportive parent to my brother and sister and me. But my dad was of no help whatsoever. It made our home life stressful.

Nora's treatment regimen began at a well-known hospital in the Midwest. She was in it only briefly, however, because our family's insurance wouldn't cover it longer than a week. So the program really didn't do her much good. In her early twenties, just as she was finishing college, she saw a psychologist who helped her learn more about being more assertive. She also went to a support group for people with eating disorders, and that helped tremendously as well. So her treatment really comprised these three areas.

But the turning point in her recovery really came when Nora received criticism at work. It was a big deal for her when her coworkers saw that something was wrong with her and she was able to see that the eating disorder was negatively affecting her job. As a result of her job change, her environment also changed to be less supportive of the eating disorder itself. It may sound like a small thing, but the cubicle and the automatic-flushing toilets really worked to take her away from the disease. These physical and environmental changes made it more difficult for the eating disorder to be in her life.

During therapy, Nora worked hard to help herself understand the eating disorder and become a stronger person. Before she started working with a counselor, I would say something hurtful to her about the eating disorder, and she'd just hang up on me. But with the help of assertiveness training, she was able to say, "Laura, don't say those things. It makes me feel bad when you say that; it really hurts my feelings." And I had no idea that I was hurting her feelings, so I changed, too. As she became more assertive, she gave voice to her feelings. She felt heard, and that was really empowering for her.

Once Nora started talking, I realized that I didn't know her at all. Now I do. Once I listened, I was able to hear who she was as a person. If I had to give advice to the family members of someone who has an eating disorder, it would be to listen. Quiet yourself, and hear what your loved one is saying.

Changing her behavior was not easy for Nora; I think she would be the first to tell you that. She struggled with body image for a long time, and that did not change right away when she began her recovery period. She had made a choice to quit bingeing and purging, and as a result, her metabolism and body shape changed a lot. She had to get rid of all her old clothes. She was on the phone with me every other night, crying. It was difficult for her, but I was glad that I could be there for her and be someone that she could trust, someone she was not afraid to call and talk to for hours.

Our relationship has changed since Nora entered recovery. We have always been close, but we are even closer now as a result of her being more assertive. She doesn't put up with any crap from me anymore. I also tread much lighter with her sensitivity and I'm more cautious about the things I say. She keeps me humble and lets me know when I am being a jerk.

And we talk about everything now. There are no secrets anymore. With the eating disorder, her life was one big secret; no one could get close to her. She's strong, she's confident, and she no longer worries about what other people think. She is an amazing woman. I am really proud of her.

Today, Nora has many friends, and they all want to do things with her. She is still shocked by the fact that people actually really like her. She is out in the world now, quite the contrast from when the eating disorder was in her life, wrapping a cocoon around her. She is happy.

## *I Forgive Myself*
## *(an affirmation)*

*I forgive myself.*
*As I forgive myself,*
*I leave behind all feelings*
*of not being good enough,*
*and I am free to love myself.*

*—Louise L. Hay*

*After my treatment was complete and I finally felt recovered, I started a whole new life of feeling… It was almost like I had shed my skin and was a whole new complete person, participating in life.*

*—Amy*

# Amy

I went on my first diet in sixth grade. Puberty was starting, and I was not ready for that kind of change. I felt uncomfortable with my body. My friends were starting to wear their first bras, and the people in my class were starting to become boyfriend and girlfriend. For me, it was unnatural; I wasn't ready for that kind of thing. I began to eat carrots and other fat-free foods. In eighth grade, I made myself vomit for the first time.

I was also in sports: tennis, softball, basketball. In high school, I was getting moved up to varsity level and I thought I had to be in perfect physical condition. I would run twice a day. It wasn't like I had to have a certain body type. It was about performance—being able to run faster, being the best, never losing.

It was also the time in my life when I was learning more about my own sexual identity, though I did not entirely understand it at the time. While the other girls in my class were trying to look cute for the boys, I was confused and anxious. My mom wanted me to wear a bra and start looking more like a girl because I was such a tomboy, but I was not comfortable with that. I did not know what to do with the feelings I was having. I came from a small town, and my parents were Catholic, so I just kind of tucked the feelings away. I think that repression had a lot to do with the eating disorder as well.

In the early stages, the eating disorder had a huge impact on my quality of life. I can remember being physically tired all the time. I was very depressed and anxious as a kid, although I did not understand it as such, and I don't think I took very good care of myself. My physical body took a toll as much as my emotional self did.

I was very strict with my diet. I would only eat fat-free food—diet soda, rice cakes, veggies, and fruit—and would get up every morning to go running. I wouldn't miss a day. I can remember going over a year on the calendar and discovering that out of those 365 days, I had not missed a day of running. And then I would go to basketball practice in the afternoon. At one point, my basketball coach intervened and talked to my dad and told him, "You just can't let her run in the morning anymore, because I can tell that her body just does not have the energy to keep performing at this high level." So my dad sat down and told me, "Amy, we have to take your running shoes away, you can't run in the morning anymore." And at that point in my life, that restriction was not an expression of caring to me; it was very threatening.

I had no notion of what good nutrition was. To me, eating fat-free foods or not eating, period, was healthy. As a result, bad eating habits became a pattern for me. I was very constipated most of the time. I was always getting stomachaches.

In ninth grade, I finally broke down and told my mom I needed help. I began to go to therapy. At first, my dad did not know how to deal with it. He denied that it existed in those early stages. And that was hard because I wanted so much to be like him in many ways.

Although I waited until high school before telling my mom about the eating disorder, my parents were not oblivious before that time. They knew something was wrong, but they couldn't pinpoint it. I was into making everyone else happy, so what I would do is just get really quiet and not talk to anyone and be a little crabby—it looked to be normal teenage stuff. They didn't know I had an eating disorder. They thought I was trying to do better for myself by being in good shape and watching what I was eating. There is such a fine line between good health habits and eating-disordered behavior. The idea that being thin is healthy is not true! If you are not educated about eating disorders, you would not be able to pick it out. And my parents couldn't pick it out until I got older.

And in the meantime, I was trying to fit in. I had a boyfriend in high school and that was horrid. I was trying to be attractive to him, and yet I didn't care. It was unfulfilling and horrible. I remember not eating anything for a week before the prom because I didn't feel comfortable in a dress. It was all so contrary to who I was. After I went to therapy a few times, I thought I was better. I began my first year in college, and I played basketball in the winter. But then when the spring hit, I had nothing else to concentrate on except the eating disorder. I was living in an apartment with someone who also had an eating disorder, and we proceeded to binge and purge together. I got into laxatives then, taking up to a box a day, and I got really sick. I was getting rid of everything I ate. That's when my family started to realize that something was really wrong. Whereas before I was maintaining a normal body shape, now I was getting way too thin, and people were starting to worry.

I remember the summer that my brother got married. I was in the wedding and I had to wear a dress, so the anxiety resurfaced. I went to the first fitting and I had already been not eating to fit into it, and I tried it on, and it was tight. And I told myself, "So, this doesn't fit? Well, it will." By the last fitting, right before the wedding, they had to get it taken in because I had lost so much weight. That's how much power my eating disorder had over me.

I had hit rock bottom. I quit school, moved home with my parents, and started working. And it was terrible. I didn't want to live with my folks, and I was so lost. My mom tried to pick me back up and help me figure it out. She sent me to a counselor, but it seemed to me to be the same old song and dance. I needed to come out. I was confused because I was in love with my best friend, yet I was denying it, and I wasn't facing the truth. I didn't know what I wanted because I was so sick. There was this huge part of my life that I wasn't dealing with, that was killing me. So I went to the therapist, and we talked, but we didn't get anything done because I wasn't telling her what I really needed to talk about. There wasn't much accomplished. I went back to school the next year, unhealed, and played basketball the following season. The eating disorder was still present, though not as actively—I wasn't throwing up every day and I exercised only sporadically—but I was depressed.

At the age of twenty-two, I had reached an impasse. Life seemed so difficult, but I didn't know why. I thought, "I'm not dumb. I have all these resources to be happy. I came from a good family. Why can't I get it together? There must be something wrong with me, and I don't know if I want to do this anymore." I literally just broke down and begged for someone to bring me somewhere for treatment, because I felt like I was going to do something harmful to myself. I was feeling suicidal, and I needed help.

I finally went to a treatment program for people with eating disorders. I felt immediately supported, and while the changes were not easy, I felt like things were set up for me to succeed. I was ready. The team approach of the program I attended offered support from different angles by a doctor, therapist, and dietitian. I had structure, being in treatment for eight hours a day and eating three meals, yet I was out in the real world just enough. I finally realized that if I didn't start trusting these people instead of my own misguided beliefs, I would not get well.

I can remember the "aha" moment when I knew I could get better. I was sitting in treatment one day and saying to myself, "Amy, you're twenty-two years old, and you don't know how to eat." And I remember right then that I had to separate myself from my eating disorder. I couldn't trust it anymore because I hadn't been happy with it. In one moment, I was saying, "Eating disorder, you suck. You are killing me. I am dying here, and I don't want you anymore."

At that point, once I had separated myself from the disease, the only thing I could think to do was to trust the people who were around me, the people who were supporting me, because I wasn't quite able to trust myself entirely. I realized that in the process of trusting others, I could also be true to myself. So one day, I just turned myself over to the process of getting well. I did everything by the book. If I was supposed to eat at five o'clock, I ate at five o'clock. I ate exactly what I was supposed to eat whether someone was watching me or not. I took responsibility for getting better—because I wanted to, and because I had to. I religiously took care of my meal plan, and I did whatever I could to give myself a good chance of feeling better. And every day, I started to feel a little bit better. There were some days where I didn't feel as great, but I would still trust. I would go a little bit further with following the treatment plan, and while I was scared, it ended up that things started happening; things started to be okay. I took everything one moment at a time, one therapy session at a time, one meal at a time. As I became better, I was more and more able to deal with the eating disorder. And I was able to admit, then, that I was questioning my sexuality. All of a sudden, I had all of these things to say. I had figured out what it was that was in my way. Within six months, I was ready to go out and live in the world. I was bound and determined to live my life without the eating disorder.

When I first came to the last treatment program, I was about 98 percent eating disorder and 2 percent Amy. Now, I am 98 percent Amy and 2 percent eating disorder. There are still tiny hints of the eating disorder that I will never get rid of, but the important thing is that I have taken over. I have all the tools to deal with the little things that come up once in a while, so it's all just standard maintenance.

The hardest part about getting better was the realization that I had to be selfish for a while, that I had to focus on me in order to get through it. Recovering meant shutting people out for a time. My family, for example, would be asking me how treatment was going, and sometimes I just did not have the energy to talk to them about it. I was devoting all my energy to recovery. I can also remember lighting a candle for myself as I was sitting down to dinner—to make the atmosphere as lovely and welcoming as possible. It was a little awkward, but it was nice. I had never before spent so much emotional energy on me. But it felt good. The eating disorder no longer had its grips on me.

After my treatment was complete and I finally felt recovered, I started a whole new life of feeling. I learned just how to wake up in the morning and journal and get to know myself and be aware. It was almost like I had shed my skin and was a whole new complete person, participating in life.

Every day, my relationships get richer and richer. I no longer have the eating disorder, so I don't have to pretend anymore. I can participate completely, and I am fully present. Because I am well, I no longer need all of the intensive support, so I can give back to my friends and family, and because I am free of the eating disorder, I can do it without feeling depleted. I don't feel anxious anymore. I feel like things are natural. I've gotten to know myself, take care of myself, be satisfied with myself, and enjoy life.

At the same time, I have anger. I have anger toward eating disorders and what they do to people's lives. My voice, which has gotten stronger over the years, says, "Don't buy into the crap, the fashion industry, the diet industry, having to look a certain way." I don't validate the negative images of women now. I speak up if I see it. Everyone goes through a lot of hard times in life, but because I experienced what I did with an eating disorder, I would never wish it upon anyone else.

I felt very hopeless when I was going through my eating disorder, so when I think about what I would tell people who are going through it today, I realize that perhaps my message will not penetrate. That said, my advice to others who are going through life with an eating disorder right now is to know that it is possible to get better. It's not easy, but you can do it. Start by asking yourself what is going on with you, right here, right this minute, and be truthful. And be aware that many, many people are surrounding you, ready to help. I attribute a great deal of my successful recovery to my parents, who love me unconditionally and supported me tirelessly as I walked my path to recovery.

It takes a lot of energy to be sick, and you have given up a lot. If you can transfer just a little bit of that energy and take some positive steps, it will take you to the other side. You can recover.

*Amy is currently living and working in Minneapolis. She is considering going back to school.*

*I believe that the struggles that we have in life are for a reason. It molds us into the people that we are today.*

*—Cheryl*

# Amy's Mom, Cheryl

Amy's eating disorder began in her early high school years. She was a very active child and involved in sports and extracurricular activities. Amy had a drive in her that no one could stop. She was a goal-setter and strived to accomplish whatever was to be endured.

As Amy's behavior began to change, it became very difficult at times to deal with her. I always seemed to rationalize her behavior and blamed it on hormones. I remember many times when Amy would wait for her dad and I to go to bed, at which time she would go downstairs to the kitchen and raid the refrigerator and cupboards. She would leave tracks everywhere in the house that would lead me to believe that she was bingeing. There were many nights that I lay awake, listening to my little girl purging in the bathroom. I remember the feelings that I was experiencing at that time. I was having many frustrating feelings because I did not know what to do. I remember waking up my husband so that he could hear her purging in the bathroom. I remember the frustration that I felt during those times as he would go right back to sleep and I would lay there for hours, hoping and praying that this would end.

During the time that Amy's eating disorder began, our family life was very chaotic. Both Amy and my son Chris were very active in three separate sports and their dad and I strived never to miss one of their special sporting or school events. Amy and Chris are very special, and my husband and I have a good relationship with both of them.

I was also very active when Amy's eating disorder began. I worked in a chiropractic office as a chiropractic assistant and was a board member with a local company. The responsibility that went along with the latter position was very time-consuming and, at times, stressful. However, I always tried to include my children when doing some of the fun things so that they would not feel excluded. During this time, I had made the decision to quit my job, go back to college, and get my degree in chemical dependency counseling.

When looking back at when Amy's eating disorder first began, I recall how Amy was able to talk to her father more about the various things that she was involved in at the time. Her father was very athletic as well, and they seemed to have a great deal in common. I always felt like I was the person in Amy's life that she had to vent her anger and frustration to. I always allowed her to talk to me inappropriately, and I recall how very hurt I would feel because I took it so personally at the time. (Later, I realized that it was not even about me.)

I believe that the eating disorder really affected Amy's life at an early age, but I am not sure at what point in her life that it became problematic. I believe the eating disorder affected my life as well because it seemed that when Amy was hurting for some reason, I would always feel that pain within myself. No one ever approached me about the eating disorder, nor did anyone in the family want to talk about it. I was feeling very alone and needing to talk to someone about my concerns and for direction in getting Amy professional help.

I recall talking to Amy about getting some help, and she did agree to see a therapist. I went with Amy to her first appointment and remember her walking out of her therapy session before it was over. Again, I was so frustrated that she was not getting anywhere.

She agreed to see a psychologist sometime after this first visit, and I believe that she did go to a few sessions, but it did not last too long, and she was back where she had started again. It was not until Amy left for college in the mid-1990s that it became quite evident that the eating disorder was really affecting her life. I remember Amy calling me at home, stating that she was really sick and needed to quit school and basketball and come home. Her life was totally out of control. She was begging for help. She was feeling as if college was not for her, and she decided to move home with her father and me. Amy began working for her father in his grocery store and did whatever she could to help him out, which he really appreciated. She worked at the store for a while and then decided to return to college once again. She continued to work at her father's store on the weekends and during the week whenever she could, and that schedule kept the two of them in contact.

About two years later, I became ill with a condition called chronic fatigue syndrome, which forced me to resign from my counseling position and left me in a bed or chair for nearly eighteen months. It was during my illness that the eating disorder really took off once again for Amy; she called home and was desperate for me to get her the help that she needed. I had all I could do to take care of myself, and now I needed to find Amy an appropriate place to be treated. At this point in Amy's life, she was having thoughts of suicide and was not feeling safe enough to be alone at all. It was at that time that she again moved home with us and we were able to talk about her feelings of hopelessness and not knowing what was going on in our lives.

I telephoned a treatment facility for people with eating disorders and left a message with the coordinator there. I will never forget this woman as long as I live, as she called me back at home and spent a great deal of time with me talking through what Amy's needs were at that time.

I did have some difficulties with being involved in Amy's treatment process because I was seeing many parallels with the eating disorder and chemical dependency. I realized that I could not do the recovery for her, and I prayed daily that she was ready to do this for herself. During the process of getting Amy into treatment, she and I had become very close. We were able to talk openly about so many things. I was so proud of her and all the hard work that she was doing in her recovery.

During the end of her treatment at the eating disorders clinic, Amy had called me to come and meet her for dinner one evening, sharing that she had something very important that she had to talk to me about. During our dinner, Amy was acting very nervous and uncomfortable until she stated that she had to tell me something. I proceeded to ask what it was that was on her mind. I will never forget this conversation that ensued.

"Mom, I am gay," she said.

I remember just glaring at her for a moment in disbelief. "How do you know that you are gay, Amy?" I asked her.

"Mom, how do you know that you are not?" she replied simply.

She shared how much of a release it was for her to finally, for the first time in her life, accept who she really is. I shared with her the fact that I have treated many gay and lesbians on a professional level—and I would have never guessed her news in a million years. I remember the emotions that came over me driving home that evening. I cried and was feeling selfish, knowing that Amy would never be getting married and believing that perhaps she would never have children of her own. I confess that I was not even thinking of the pain that she was going through in just being able to "come out" for the first time with her mom.

I knew then that Amy really trusted me because she felt comfortable enough to share this information with me. I knew that things were going to be difficult as we told family members. But one thing was for certain: I loved Amy with all of my heart, and nothing would ever change that. I realized that Amy had not changed but that people's perception of her had. It was difficult for me to share the news with others in the beginning, as I was fearful they would reject her. Eventually, however, my ability to be forthcoming about it helped family members discuss it more openly. Through it all, Amy's and my relationship became stronger and stronger. I love my daughter unconditionally, and I will stand by her until the day we part from this world. I felt a peace within Amy when she told me she was gay. My daughter was finally healing and accepting the person that she truly is.

I had a wonderful support system during this very difficult period. My family stood by me, and I have so many wonderful friends with whom I was able to talk so openly and honestly. The experience also taught me who my true friends are—the ones who were there for me in good times and bad and would love me without question.

There were changes that I knew I had to make for myself. I was trying to control a situation over which I had no control. I always wanted to be able to help my children in any way I could, and I knew for the first time that I could not heal Amy. She had to get through these challenges by herself—and in her own time.

Shortly after Amy got through treatment, she received a speeding ticket and came home to see if I would help her pay it off, as she did not have the money. I remember so well the anger and frustration that I was feeling at the time. I agreed to pay the ticket for her but also told her that I had to be paid back for it. When Amy left our home that day, I told myself, "This is the end! I will no longer continue to carry her through all of these things." I proceeded to write her a letter and told her that I was done enabling her and that from now on she had to fall and feel the consequences of her behavior.

I feared the fact that I had taken a risk with Amy for the first time in my life and that she was going to be very angry with me. I was correct, and she did not speak to me for three weeks. When Mother's Day came, I was so worried that I would not even hear from her. But she arrived at my mother-in-law's for brunch with flowers and a beautiful card, and she sat next to me during the meal. When she grabbed my hand and held it under the table the whole time we were eating, I felt the healing process in her. We both felt such peace with one another. I was not able to read the card until I got home because I knew that I would fall apart. I proceeded to read it when I got home; it was so beautifully written, and it remains close to me so I can read it every day. That day was a turning point in Amy's life and in her recovery process.

Amy is doing very well. She is finding out who she really is and is liking the person that she has become. She has become stronger and stronger as a person, and I am so proud of her and feel blessed to have her as my daughter and true friend.

The question was asked, "What have you lost because of the eating disorder?" I do not feel that I have lost anything. I am a very positive person, and I try to bring appreciation to everything in my life. I feel that the eating disorder has made me a much stronger person. I was given the tools and the knowledge to cope with Amy's illness, and the rest was totally up to me. I was taught that I really need to take care of myself, and for the first time in my entire life, I have been doing so and I feel free. I have regained my health and a relationship with my daughter, who I truly adore. Amy is an inspiration and a true gift of life.

I have always told Amy that I hope she never forgets the very difficult times with the eating disorder, as it is a constant reminder of where she was in life and how far she has come in her recovery process. I believe that the struggles that we have in life are for a reason. It molds us into the people that we are today.

Amy was given a "tool box" during her treatment. I am grateful that she has put her tools to work; it will allow her to help others.

For the supporters of those individuals who have an eating disorder, the only advice that I would give is to take good care of yourselves and unconditionally love the person who is struggling with the eating disorder. And never, ever give up hope.

## *How Could Anyone*

*How could anyone ever tell you*

*You were anything less than beautiful?*

*How could anyone ever tell you*

*You were less than whole?*

*How could anyone fail to notice*

*That your loving is a miracle?*

*How deeply you're connected to my soul.*

*—Libby Roderick*
*songwriter and lyricst*
*(song performed by*
*Trish Bruxvoort Colligan)*

*I think recovery continues to be a daily occurrence, by way of those little moments where I can take a deep breath and have such gratitude for being in good health...I inhale and exhale and say thank you to myself even for deciding to be well.*

*—Hannah*

# Hannah

I can trace the beginning of my eating disorder all the way back to grade school. In fact, even before it took shape, I was immersed in disordered eating behavior. It was practically in my blood.

I grew up in a family where the women were always on a diet. At mealtimes, my mother and grandmother would measure food at the table and talk about this class or that class that they were attending in order to lose weight. And it became just a given for me that dieting was what women in my family do. Weight is never stable; yo-yo dieting is the norm. We weigh our food at the table and ourselves on the scale, and we are never satisfied with our bodies.

When I was about ten years old, my grandmother challenged me to a diet to see who could be the first person to lose ten pounds. And it was this crazy "lose-ten-pounds-in-a-week" diet. I remember taking to school, in my Pink Panther lunch box, four saltine crackers and a half-cup of cottage cheese and my little carton of milk. That's what I would eat for lunch. And it turned out that I was really good at losing weight and I won the challenge with my grandmother. And I think that the reward was something incredibly ironic, like a trip to Dairy Queen or something. So I learned to lose weight by severely restricting my diet. I learned I could do it well and get lots of affirmation for it and then be rewarded by bingeing. Although I had witnessed this same behavior in my mother and grandmother, I did not actually follow suit until that point. But once I restricted my diet and felt the unnatural high that comes from losing weight, I picked it up on my own and began doing it. And for about three years, it was that sort of pattern—extreme restriction and then bingeing. By the age of thirteen, when I was in eighth grade, I saw a counselor and psychiatrist for the first time, and they picked up immediately that I had an eating disorder. Slowly, in the course of a few months, I stopped the bingeing and started severely restricting my food intake. Shortly before my fourteenth birthday, I was in treatment for eating disorders.

It was amazing that someone was able to recognize it back then, from a clinical standpoint. The treatment center itself was new and probably not as good as some, but it was a place to begin. Because of insurance and all sorts of other things, I was there for two weeks and then was sent home. It was very clear to me that I had gotten only a tiny bit of what I needed to become healthy. I was sent back into this family that, in addition to having all sorts of weight issues, had its own brand and degree of dysfunction that I suppose every family has in some respect. But it was not a place where I could find recovery. I went home learning new tricks. (For instance, I had become constipated in the hospital, and my doctor gave me laxatives to improve the constipation. I lied and told my parents I needed to continue using them, so they ended up buying them for me, and I abused the medications.) I was in treatment again that following summer and then again about a year later.

As I entered high school, and perhaps even before then, it became clear that there was no place for me to find lasting recovery in my family. In a very real sense, I was living in an environment that was not conducive to healing. As the oldest of four children, I was expected, on many levels, to fend for myself—and to grow up without the emotional support of my parents. Consequently, my mother and father were very disinterested in my life and what's important to me.

Physical punishment was also part of the daily discipline routine in my home. My parents grew up in a strict, fundamentalist Christian Reformed Church that actively encouraged spanking and corporal punishment of children—the "spare the rod, spoil the child" mentality—and they continued this tradition with their children.

Looking back, I see that my parents were also at a loss to deal with my full-spectrum vision of the world. Although not manic in a clinical sense, I was always a bit larger than life; a performer even from a very young age, my dramatic flair was too much for their religiously rigid, do-the-right-thing, never-call-attention-to-yourself world. But I wanted to be seen, known, and understood. Their lack of acceptance left me feeling a deep sadness that, throughout my childhood (and sometimes still), I experienced as low-grade melancholy to bouts of depression.

By my junior year in high school, I was at a very low weight and still really struggling with the eating disorder. It was clear that one way or another, the eating disorder was killing me.

When I was sixteen, I attempted suicide. Following this attempt, while I was still in the hospital, my mother called the Department of Human Services and said she and my father didn't want me to live with them anymore. They felt they had done all they could and my lack of recovery was adversely affecting the whole family. Their way to deal with this destruction was to remove me from the picture.

While I was in the hospital, a social worker came to see me and said, "You need to be out of your family. This is not healthy." She said the first objective is always to keep a child with the family and begin with individual and family therapy. However, she saw that my home environment was so hostile to my health and my parents were so adamant that I could not come home, that home was not a good place for me. And I think teachers at school and other people at church had seen this for a long time, but it had to take something that drastic to make people really take action. So in my junior year of high school, the week before Thanksgiving, I went to a foster home. It was a wonderful experience, and it saved my life. It was like going into residential treatment. At that time, my eating disorder was so wound into my being that I could not separate it from who I really was. My foster family was able to help me tease that out and say that the eating disorder was part of me but was not me. They were most accustomed to caring for medically needy babies, so initially, they were reluctant to have a teenager in the house. But it ended up being a great match. They loved me and really gave me a place to heal. When I was in foster care, I met with a therapist twice weekly and with my psychiatrist monthly (for regulation of medications).

I know that my parents did the best they could, but even today, I question whether they ever understood what recovery would look like for me, or what their role in my recovery would be. I think they thought if they could just get me out, all would go back to "normal." I think they wanted to think that the eating disorder was just about food, so some of the things they did to attempt to support me revolved around food. For instance, even with four kids, my family got groceries only once a month. It was a big event to make that visit to the store, and also a big production, as you can imagine, because they would walk out of the supermarket with an enormous amount of food. When I was done with that first round of treatment, they came to me as they were making their grocery list and said, "What foods do you need for your meal plan?" I would put down some "safe" foods on the list—bagels, yogurt. But that's as involved as they got with the food aspect. I can remember my mother reading a couple of books and going to a couple of classes, then coming home feeling like she and my dad didn't need more help, that this was my issue, not theirs. And that notion was true to some extent, but as a fourteen-year-old dependent, I really felt like recovery had to involve the whole family, and my parents could never make that connection. I think they still don't make that connection. They could never take responsibility for the illness aspect or the recovery. So while they wanted to support me, I don't think they were ever able to.

The treatment facility that I was in was actually part of a psychiatric unit at a smaller hospital near my hometown. The thing that I took away from it was that recovery is about choices. I remember thinking, "Oh, I get it now! No one makes me feel a certain way; I choose how I feel when something happens at school or with my relationships." So the greatest gift from treatment was understanding choices and feelings.

Another thing that was helpful—not during treatment, but after it—was going to my foster home. When my foster family made a meal, I would not only eat what was there, I would also watch what this healthy family ate—to help gauge what was "normal." They had tater tots; they had Ramen noodles. They had yogurt and fruit. They even had a candy drawer. There was very little stress around meals and meal planning in my foster home—no scales, no diets, just eating in a moderate fashion. How they could eat a variety of foods and still be healthy was amazing to me—and radically different than how things were with my own family. In my family, food was either in excess, or in my case, it was nothing. It was so vital to me to be integrated into my foster family and see how a normal, healthy family treated food and dealt with their emotions and anger and conversation. They also really embraced me, which was profoundly healing.

I look back and am amazed at how successful I was in creating a circle of support around myself. Somehow I knew on an instinctive level that I needed to open up to others in order to survive. In addition to my foster family, I had my social worker, who handled all the human services aspects of my situation. I had a therapist whom I met with twice weekly. For spiritual support, I met once a week with the pastor of my family's church. And I had the continual support of one of the school guidance counselors. (He was such a shining light; I would often go to his office just to do my homework.) All of those people were so key in helping me recover. And each person represented something significant to me.

I had good friends during that time, too. All but one of them were older than I was, but for me, I always felt like in a small town, I had this big, strange story and people knew about it. And I think most of the kids my age were kind of afraid of me.

My foster family had said that if I stayed with them until I graduated from high school, they would "emotionally adopt" me—I could always go back to them and they would help me with college. And while that was very important to me, I felt like I had to give my family of origin another chance. I knew I couldn't just walk away. I had siblings who were younger than me. I had aunts and uncles and grandparents whom I still wanted to see, and I needed to find out if those relationships could heal. So when I was eighteen, against the advice of nearly everyone I knew, I moved out on my own, rented an apartment a block from high school, bought a car, got an after-school job, and directed the children's choir at my church. I was doing all of the things that you normally wouldn't do as a late-teen. I also began limited contact with my family. During that time, I did struggle a bit with my eating disorder because I was shopping for myself and doing all these things I had to do for myself that I hadn't done before. And yet, I did really okay with it all; I had a few slips but no major relapse.

About a year after moving out on my own, I met a pastor who was organizing a worship band that needed a lead singer. He was nineteen years my senior. We started spending time together, then dated, and eventually, we became engaged. The relationship was not a healthy one. As often happens in relationships, I chose a partner for myself that reflected the atmosphere of my family of origin. He was an angry alcoholic who wanted to control me. He wanted me to change my body by undergoing liposuction and breast augmentation. (I was not overweight, just badly shaped, in his opinion.) He was willing to pay for it and said it would make me a better performer (with a better body, I would be more appealing to the masses). Two weeks before the wedding, he called it off. During that whole period, I began to realize for myself, "This is not okay that he wants me to be something different than I am." But I couldn't claim my body or my life for what it was, nor could I see it as a gift that the marriage did not come to be. I couldn't understand how I could find myself in this relationship with someone who wanted me to be so drastically different than who I was.

In time—about eighteen months after the wedding was called off—I did claim my body with its lumps and bumps and cellulite and all that it was—and all that he wanted me to change about myself. When I was able to claim all of what made up my body and when I was able to work with my body, I was able to reach a deeper level of recovery. I knew then that I was not just eating so that I wouldn't have to go back to the hospital. There was an emotional place in me that said, "I get it. I get to feed not only my body but also my emotions and spirit, too. And I get to accept this body with all its good and bad, and it's the only thing that's mine." That wasn't just a moment, that was a journey—to get to that place of higher self-respect and self-love.

And I still am on that journey. Even though it's been years now, I have tiny little insights and epiphanies that add up, over the course of the years, to "this is my body." My body has had a baby now, and it's still my body. I hope throughout my entire life, I will get to love myself more and more. I like myself more on some days than others, which I guess is what everyone goes through.

(How amazing for me to sit here and say that everyone goes through what I am going through! I am now part of the constituency that is making healthy choices rather than extreme ones.)

After that moment when I realized that eating meant more than just staying out of the hospital, my relationships changed a lot. There was first this physical recovery where I knew that I had to eat to live. Then there was the emotional aspect—that I get to care not just for my body, but for my emotions. And I feel like it was shortly after that that there was more of a spiritual component to my healing. All the parts of me lined up—body, mind, and spirit. During that journey of being engaged to this pastor, being in this emotionally and sexually abusive relationship with him yet having my life so linked to his, and then having the marriage called off, I still was able to heal. I did that for myself, and it just wowed me. When I told myself, "I will not be treated unlovingly by anyone in my life," when I understood that about myself, that's when I knew that something was drastically different for the better. I was not only surviving; I was thriving. I was eating because I wanted to be whole and alive in the world.

Having grown up in a very strict fundamentalist, Bible-based tradition with my family, it was strange to be coming right up against questions like, "How could God let this happen?" I felt like I had been in crisis after crisis, and I did not know what that meant in terms of my understanding of God. I met other women who were abused by clergy and they had turned away from the church, and I felt for the first time in my life that perhaps this was all right—and that God thought it was all right. Whereas before what defined spirituality for me was the notion that Jesus was your ticket into heaven—more about everlasting life and less about the present—the "here and now" became really important to me. I grew up believing only for the assurance of life beyond this life. But then what about this life? For me, faith—or spirituality—has needed to become an everyday occurrence in order to make sense.

As a result of this shift in thinking, I explored other traditions—Native American prayers, Buddhist meditations—and I found that they nourished me. And so the challenge then became how to integrate those traditions into my current faith and understand that there is so much more color in the world than just this black-and-white, life-and-death notion. And that became a great awakening for me. I was feeding my body, nurturing my emotions, and then I was awakening to a whole new way of spirituality. I found that meditation and contemplative prayer only add to my sense of recovery and that body, mind, and spirit are all connected. To name it otherwise—that recovery is all about the food—is to block out all the other colors of a person's life. And there is just a wealth of experience to integrate into recovery.

My family of origin is very musical. My father loves to sing, and when I was in fifth grade, I wrote my first song. I found that this was a wonderful outlet for me—writing music and poetry. After school every day, when I returned to my foster care home, I would go to the music room to play the piano and sing. Music continues to serve as my livelihood, but it's also how I process my healing and share my story. Sometimes when I am doing concerts for junior high kids, the journey of my recovery becomes important to share, not so much for the drama of it, but because everyone has a story and almost everyone knows someone who has an eating disorder. It is hopeful for kids and parents to see and hear a person who has been in recovery for twelve years.

There was not one moment when I thought I was recovered. I think recovery continues to be a daily occurrence, by way of those little moments where I can take a deep breath and have such gratitude for being in good health. Sure, I still have fifteen pounds to lose after my pregnancy, but I am healthy; I am making wise choices. And I am sometimes very amazed that I am as healthy as I am. So I inhale and exhale and say thank you to myself even for deciding to be well.

I have been married now for nearly five years. A musician himself, Randy and I met through the circle of our music work. He is the kindest, most compassionate person I know, and his deep love for me often catches me by surprise. Randy celebrates my life, loves my body, and affirms the core of who I am. And while I consider this to be a soulmate relationship, it still takes a great deal of work! But I am up to the challenge of this work. It's the substance of soul work. It's the journey to even greater self-awareness and healing. Together, we are parents to our two-year-old son, which makes our life together even more interesting and wondrous. It's never boring.

In the passage of my recovery, I have received a gift, and it's something that I want to pass on. I want to be a voice in other women's lives, whatever their journey. There are not enough places in the world where people feel listened to and are heard for who they are. Simply attending to people's stories can often be just what they need to begin trusting their own path in life.

There is very little that has been untouched by my experience with eating disorders and the shift that has occurred in my life. I am surprised, touched, grateful, and even a bit scared, but open. Open to what my life is teaching me. And that is what I want to help others understand—that each part of a person's story is a great gift. It is what makes us whole as human beings. It is what fills our lives and bodies with wonder and beauty.

*Hannah is now twenty-nine years old. She continues her work as a full-time songwriter and musician. She also works as a spiritual director. Having served women in private practice since 1999, she is currently advancing her training at a spiritual center in Saint Paul, Minnesota. Hannah conducts retreats for women—encouraging them to connect with their body, mind, and spirit and reminding them that their journey toward wholeness shall always be respected.*

# The Invitation

*It doesn't interest me what you do for a living. I want to know what you*
*ache for, and if you dare to dream of meeting your heart's longing.*

*It doesn't interest me how old you are. I want to know if you will risk*
*looking like a fool for love, for your dream, for the adventure of being alive.*

*It doesn't interest me what planets are squaring your moon.*
*I want to know if you have touched the center of your own sorrow,*
*if you have been opened by life's betrayals or have become shriveled and*
*closed from fear of further pain! I want to know if you can sit with pain,*
*mine or your own, without moving to hide it or fade it or fix it.*

*I want to know if you can be with joy, mine or your own,*
*if you can dance with wildness and let the ecstasy fill you to the tips of your*
*fingers and toes without cautioning us to be careful, to be realistic,*
*to remember the limitations of being human.*

*It doesn't interest me if the story you are telling me is true.*
*I want to know if you can disappoint another to be true to yourself;*
*if you can bear the accusation of betrayal and not betray your own soul;*
*if you can be faithless and therefore trustworthy.*

*I want to know if you can see beauty, even when it's not pretty,*
*every day, and if you can source your own life from its presence.*

*I want to know if you can live with failure, yours and mine, and still stand*
*on the edge of the lake and shout to the silver of the full moon, "Yes!"*

*It doesn't interest me to know where you live or how much money you have.*
*I want to know if you can get up, after the night of grief and despair, weary*
*and bruised to the bone, and do what needs to be done to feed the children.*

*It doesn't interest me who you know or how you came to be here. I want to*
*know if you will stand in the center of the fire with me and not shrink back.*

*It doesn't interest me where or what or with whom you have studied. I want*
*to know what sustains you, from the inside, when all else falls away.*

*I want to know if you can be alone with yourself and if you*
*truly like the company you keep in the empty moments.*

*—Oriah Mountain Dreamer*

# Resources on Eating Disorders

**About-Face**
P.O. Box 77665
San Francisco, CA 94107
(415) 436-0212
*www.about-face.org*

**Academy for Eating Disorders**
6728 Old McLean Village Drive
McLean, VA 22101
(703) 556-9222
*www.aedweb.org*

**Anna Westin Foundation**
112329 Chatfield Court
Chaska, MN 55318
(952) 361-3051
*www.annawestinfoundation.org*

**Anorexia Nervosa and Related Eating Disorders**
*www.anred.com*

**Dads & Daughters**
34 East Superior Street #200
Duluth, MN 55802
(888) 824-DADS
*www.dadsanddaughters.org*

**Eating Disorders Coalition**
611 Pennsylvania Avenue SE #423
Washington, DC 20003
(202) 543-9570
*www.eatingdisorderscoalition.org*

**Gurze Books**
P.O. Box 2238
Carlsbad, CA 92018
(800) 756-7533
*www.gurze.com*

**International Eating Disorder Referral Organization**
2923 Sandy Pointe #6
Del Mar, CA 92014
(858) 792-7463
*www.edreferral.com*

**Eating Disorders Institute Methodist Hospital**
6490 Excelsior Boulevard
St. Louis Park, MN 55426
(800) 862-7412 ext. 6200
(952) 993-6200
*www.parknicollet.com/edi*

**National Association of Anorexia Nervosa and Associated Disorders**
P.O. Box 7
Highland Park, IL 60035
(847) 831-3438
*www.anad.org*

**National Eating Disorders Association**
603 Stewart Street #803
Seattle, WA 98101
(206) 382-3587
*www.nationaleatingdisorders.org*

# Recommended Reading

Andersen, Arnold; Cohn, Leigh; and Holbrook, Thomas. ***Making Weight: Healing Men's Conflicts with Food, Weight, Shape and Appearance.*** Carlsbad, CA: Gurze Books, 2000.

Berg, Frances M. ***Women Afraid to Eat: Breaking Free in Today's Weight-Obsessed World.*** Hettinger, ND: Healthy Weight Network, 2001.

Berg, Frances M. ***Children and Teens Afraid to Eat: Helping Youth in Today's Weight-Obsessed World.*** Hettinger, ND: Healthy Weight Network, 2001.

Cooke, Kaz. ***Real Gorgeous: The Truth About Body and Beauty.*** New York: W.W. Norton & Company, 1996.

Freedman, Rita. ***Body Love: Learning to Like Our Looks and Ourselves.*** Calsbad, CA: Gurze Books, 2002.

Friedman, Sandra Susan. ***When Girls Feel Fat: Helping Girls Through Adolescence.*** Buffalo, NY: Firefly Books, 2000.

Institute for Research and Education HealthSystem Minnesota. ***How Did This Happen? A Practical Guide to Understanding Eating Disorders—for Teachers, Parents and Coaches.*** Minneapolis: Park Nicollet HealthSource, 1999. (For orders, please call (800) 862-7412, ext. 6555.)

Johnston, Anita. ***Eating by the Light of the Moon.*** Carlsbad, CA: Gurze Books, 2000.

Maine, Margo. ***Body Wars: Making Peace with Women's Bodies.*** Carlsbad, CA: Gurze Books, 2000.

Pipher, Mary. ***Hunger Pains: The Modern Woman's Tragic Quest for Thinness.*** New York: Ballantine Books, 1997.

Satter, Ellyn. ***Secrets of Feeding a Healthy Family.*** Madison, WI: Kelcy Press, 1999.

# Acknowledgments

This book was developed by Methodist Hospital Eating Disorders Institute in Minneapolis, Minnesota. Funding support was provided by proceeds raised from the 1998 Celebration for Life Gala, a benefit for the Eating Disorders Institute, which was sponsored by the Park Nicollet Foundation.

This book was edited by Jane Norstrom, MA; Cindy Schallock, BA; and Shannon Simper, MBA, of Methodist Hospital Eating Disorders Institute. The editors wish to gratefully acknowledge the courage of everyone who shared their stories in these pages and made this book possible. We also wish to thank the reviewers of this manuscript: Jill Gorius, MD; Chris Johnson, MD; Susan Reynolds, MSW, LICSW; and Carol Tappen, BA.

Finally, we extend our sincere gratitude to J Campbell, of Artville, Inc., for creating the cover design, illustrations, and layout for this book; to Jeanne Mettner, MA, ELS, of Planetary Ink, for her editing and production management; to Kathie Harrison, for her transcription work; and to LaVonne Meyer, for her superb proofreading of this manuscript.

The stories in this book are true. The names and identifying information have been changed to protect the privacy of the contributors. This book cannot serve as a substitute for treatment of eating disorders. Material in this publication is for general information only and is not intended to provide specific advice or recommendations for any individual. Always consult your doctor for advice concerning your own situation or illness.

# Permissions and Credits

The authors have made every effort to trace the ownership of all copyrighted materials in this volume and believe that all necessary permissions have been secured. If any errors or omissions have inadvertently been made, proper corrections will gladly be made in future editions.

Thanks are due to the following authors, publishers, publications, and agents for permission to use the material included:

"The Journey" by Mary Oliver. From *Dream Work.* © 1986 by Mary Oliver. Reprinted by permission of Grove/Atlantic, Inc., and the author.

"The Invitation" by Oriah Mountain Dreamer. From *The Invitation.* © 1999 by Oriah Mountain Dreamer. Reprinted by permission of HarperCollins Publishers, Inc., and the author.

Excerpt from Katie's journals. Printed by permission of the author.

"I Forgive Myself" affirmation. From *Power Thought Cards.* © 1999 by Louise L. Hay. Reprinted by permission of Hay House, Inc., Carlsbad, CA, and the author.

"How Could Anyone," words and music by Libby Roderick. © 1998 by Libby Roderick Music. All rights reserved. From the recording "If You See a Dream." Turtle Island Records, (907) 278-6817; www.alaska.net/~libbyr/

"Trust in yourself to know what is right…" by Christine. Printed by permission of the author.

## About the Editors

***Jane Norstrom*** is director of Methodist Hospital Eating Disorders Institute in Minneapolis, Minnesota. Her work at the Institute is focused on research, education, outreach, and development. She is continually exploring new ways to improve the programs and materials available for patients and families living with eating disorders. She feels privileged to be part of a mission to make eating disorders an illness of the past.

Jane lives in Plymouth, Minnesota. She spends much of her free time at her cabin in Northern Minnesota.

***Cindy Schallock*** is outreach coordinator at Methodist Hospital Eating Disorders Institute. She plans, creates, and facilitates conferences and community in-services on eating disorders. She also assists in the development of videos and programs on eating disorders which allow her to help other individuals recognize, address, and even prevent eating disorders.

Cindy lives in Chanhassen, Minnesota, with her husband. She has one son, age twenty-two, and two daughters, ages nineteen and sixteen.

***Shannon Simper*** is a health educator at Methodist Hospital Eating Disorders Institute. Through her work, she has had the good fortune to meet and speak with youth and adults in the community to increase awareness of eating disorders. Her interest in program development and education enables her to play a vital role in the creation of programs and materials that help parents, teachers, coaches, and students identify and prevent eating disorders.

Shannon lives in Saint Louis Park, Minnesota, with her eight-year-old daughter and three-year-old son.

**Methodist Hospital**

Eating Disorders Institute

*Methodist Hospital Eating Disorders Institute provides specialized services for the primary prevention, early intervention, and treatment of eating disorders, utilizing a multidisciplinary, team-care approach across a comprehensive continuum of care, including outpatient, intensive outpatient, partial day hospital, inpatient, and residential care settings.*

**Eating Disorders Institute**
**6490 Excelsior Boulevard**
**Saint Louis Park, MN 55426**
**952-993-6200**